NAVY AIR COLORS

United States Navy, Marine Corps, And Coast Guard Aircraft Camouflage and Markings Vol. 1 1911-1945

Thomas E. Doll   **Berkley R. Jackson**

William A. Riley

illustrated by Don Greer

Squadron/Signal Publications

Two SB2U-2 "Vindicators" of Bombing Two returning to USS Lexington ahead of the gathering storm, July, 1939.

ISBN 0-89747-143-1

If you have any photographs of the aircraft, armor, soldiers or ships of any nation, particularly wartime snapshots, why not share them with us and help make Squadron/Signal's books all the more interesting and complete in the future. Any photograph sent to us will be copied and the original returned. The donor will be fully credited for any photos used. Please send them to: Squadron/Signal Publications, Inc., 1115 Crowley Dr., Carrollton, TX 75011-5010.

ACKNOWLEDGEMENTS

We are deeply indebted to the following individuals for their assistance during the preparation of this work. Included are some of the finest and most respected names in the field of aviation history. These dedicated gentlemen gave of their time and resources to make this book as complete as possible at this point in time.

A Special mention must be made regarding the extra effort and contributions of the following five men. Our project could not have started without them.

Harold Andrews
Harry Gann
Rowland P. Gill
William T. Larkins
Arthur Schoeni
Thank you very much...

RAdm. Frank Akers, USN, Ret.
A.J. Bibee
Peter M. Bowers
Stan Brown
John W. Caler
Dustin W. Carter
Ramon Class
Joseph Consiglio
Capt. L.E. Dailey, USMC
Fred C. Dickey
Bude Donato
James Dresser
Major John Elliot, USMC, Ret.
James C. Fahey
Edward T. Garvey
Goodyear Tire & Rubber Co.
LCdr. J.W. Green
Grumman Aircraft & Eng. Co.
Thomas C. Haywood
Clay Jansson
M.J. Kishpaugh
C.E. Krischano
Robert Lawson
Paul R. Matt
Edward McCollum
Ray Minnear

W. C. Munkasy
National Archives & Records Center
Gregory Nikola
Stan Norris
Cdr. H.S. Packard, USN. Ret.
Lee M. Pearson
Pensacola NAS Photo Lab
LCdr. J.M. Pierce, USNR
Wilford Ransom
Richard Sailer
San Diego Aerospace Museum
Capt. W.E. Scarborough, USN, Ret.
Roger Seybil
Silver Eagles/San Diego Wing
Smithsonian Institution
Spence Air Photos
William Steed
William Swisher
Adm. J.S. Thach, USN, Ret.
Edward K. Turner
USCG Public Information Office
USMC Historical Branch
D. Bruce Van Alstine
Clarke Van Vleet
Adrian O. Van Wyen
Gordon S. Williams

DEDICATION

To that largely anonymous group of amateur photographers whose documentation of planes, people, and places constitutes an invaluable contribution to the history of aviation.

INTRODUCTION

Of all the facets of aviation history; painting schemes, national insignia, organizational markings, unit badges, and personal emblems are the most difficult to document. Specifications, Technical Orders, Letters, and Memoranda are basic sources of data. Photographs and personal recollections, while mostly supportive, are often contradictory and/or misleading, if not viewed as variations to the norm.

Implementation of official directives issued by the Bureau of Aeronautics and Fleet and Force Commanders could take months to become effective. Unit custom and/or command perrogatives resulted in variations that were sometimes major in scope. Many of these will be noted in the text and photographically.

From the procurement of its first aircraft in 1911, through World War One, Navy and Marine Corps aviation was almost entirely coast based. Seaplanes (695) and flying boats (1,170) far outnumbered the 242 landplanes on hand on 11 November 1918. In general, color was basic and markings were simple.

The slow but steady growth between the two World Wars took landplanes to sea aboard aircraft carriers and placed float planes on all battleships and cruisers. Continuing organizational changes were a natural result, with corresponding changes in color and markings. The tremendous expansion during World War Two brought major changes in painting schemes and for a time, a near disappearance of unit markings.

In consideration of these variables, therefore, the authors have attempted to describe the evolution of the color schemes and markings carried by aircraft and airships of the United States Navy, Marine Corps, and Coast Guard from 1911 through 1945. In so doing, every effort has been made to correlate the "official" with the "visual" record and to resolve the many ambiguities thereby disclosed.

EARLY DAYS,
WORLD WAR I AND THE GOLDEN AGE

The color and finish applied to the first aircraft acquired by the U.S. Navy, was similiar to that used in aircraft constructed for sale to private individuals. The general practice of the period (1911-1915) was to apply four or five coats of clear dope to the fabric covering the aerodynamic surface and fuselage. Varnish, or sometimes paint, was then applied to prevent the fabric from becoming damp and stretching. The wooden parts of the airframe were painted or varnished to inhibit warping and the absorption of moisture. Metal fittings and control wires were painted or varnished to reduce the effects of corrosion.

These protective finishes were essential to the preservation of the airplane's aerodynamic and structural qualities, and extended its life by protecting it from deterioration. Fabric covered areas were an off-White or Light Tan color, while struts, floats, and hulls were varying shades of varnish or paint.

Color made an appearance in 1915, both on the hulls of flying boats and hydro aeroplanes, with experiments in the use of high visibility color schemes in the case of aircraft operating from ships. It was not until late in 1916, however, that color came into general use. N-9's acquired from Curtiss and Burgess were finished in a pigmented varnish, opaque Yellow in color, ranging from Cream to bright Yellow. This finish probably was adopted from that being applied to aircraft built by Curtiss for the British.

Painting specifications of mid-1917 called for Curtiss-built aircraft to be finished with English Khaki-Gray enamel in lieu of opaque Yellow, and its use was extended to other manufacturers. This was followed by a Gray pontoon enamel which, despite its name, was applied to some complete aircraft. The requirement for a low-visibility finish resulted in the issuance of Aerospecification No. 7 on 6 March 1918, entitled: "Specification for Naval Gray Pontoon Enamel".

While overall painting in Naval Gray became the standard finish in 1918, considerable variation in color schemes was apparent. Procurement problems in a period of changing standards resulted in composite color schemes of Khaki Gray and Naval Gray. Since no attempt was made to achieve uniformity of color by repainting, both colors existed until well after the end of World War I.

Various tests of high visibility and camouflage painting schemes were conducted during 1916-20. A Burgess-Dunne was given a "dazzle" finish in irregular light and dark shades, and the Curtiss AH-18 was painted in a checker-board pattern of alternating light and dark squares. A number of randrom camouflage schemes can be noted from a study of photographs.

Although it was not until May of 1917 that the United States Army adopted standard military aircraft markings, U.S. Navy aircraft were identified as such shortly after procurement of the first three in 1911. This marking usually was applied in block letters (i.e. U.S.N) with the combined type-serial (i.e. AH-15) placed below. Considerable variation in placement, even on aircraft of the same type, was common. Frequent rebuilding of the "bam-boo tail" AH-type and the variance in configuration of the other aircraft on hand precluded standardization.

In late 1916, a Blue anchor replaced the "U.S.N." marking and was usually applied to each side of the rudder. Again, variation in placement was common. The anchor was enclosed in a circle on the Sturtevant Model S seaplane at the Rhode Island Naval Militia, while on the Richardson "Twin", the shank of the anchor was applied along the hinge of the rudder and vertical fin. Curtiss N-9s, photographed at Pensacola in January of 1917, carried the anchor on the underside of the lower wing-tips and both sides of the rudder.

A standard national marking, for both Army and Navy aircraft was adopted in May of 1917. Related to the national markings used on aircraft of the Allied powers, it consisted of a White five-pointed star imposed on a Blue circle, with a Red disc centered on the star. At first, placement of this marking was inboard of the ailerons, spanning the full chord of the upper and lower wings. As with previous markings, variations in size and placement were extensive. At the same time, a rudder marking was prescribed; three equally spaced vertical stripes, with Blue at the rudder post, then White, and Red.

The order of the tail stripes was reversed at the request of the Allies in January of 1918, and the wing marking was replaced by a tri-color circle with Red on the outside, then Blue, and a White center. While this presentation continued in effect until August of 1919, some U.S. Navy aircraft operating in the United States retained the old markings and, in a few instances, carried combinations of both old and new.

The painting directive of 19 May, 1917, also contained instructions for the placement of the aircraft serial number, stating: "the building number of each aircraft shall be placed in figures 3" high on each side of the rudder at the top of the White band hereinbefore mentioned." By this time, the letter-number system to designate aircraft type and serial number had been replaced by serial numbers issued in direct sequence of procurement. An "A" for aeroplane, preceeded the three or four digit number. In accordance with an amendment of the order, the serial number was applied in large block figures on each side of the fuselage or hull. A dash was usually placed between the "A" and the figures, but this was often omitted, as was the "A" itself. Fuselage application was usually in White paint, but Black was not uncommon.

Overseas in World War I, the U.S. Navy operated flying boats and seaplanes from a total of 20 bases in England, Ireland, France and Italy. On U.S. built flying boats, the large fuselage serial number was sometimes replaced by equally large letter-numbers, indicating the station and aircraft

Curtiss AH-1 damaged at San Diego in 1912. U.S.N. in large block letters appeared on both undersurfaces and was repeated in smaller White lettering on the dark colored tail. (USN via R.L. Lawson)

4

Curtiss C-3 (later AB-3) on a cruiser catapult at Pensacola, July 1916. Anchor first appeared in 1916 but was not applied to all aircraft. (USN via H.S. Gann)

number. (i.e., LV-12 for the 12th aircraft assigned to L'Abner Vrack Air Station). Allied equipment utilized by the U.S. Navy retained original finish when operated from overseas bases.

Aircraft of the U.S. Marine Corps observed Navy directives in the application of finish and markings. In what appears to be one of the first uses of the Corps globe and anchor divice, the emblem was applied to the DH-4/DH-9A aircraft of the Day Wing of the Northern Bombing Group. In this instance, the "globe" was soon replaced by the Red-Blue-White tri-color wing marking. In addition, the four squadrons of the Wing were identified by a letter-number applied to the vertical fin (i.e., D-5 for the 5th aircraft in Squadron D).

Possibly, because there was no squadron organization in Naval aviation at the time, there is little evidence of unit insignia. However, photographs do confirm the use of insignia at Pensacola and Miami, as well as one-of-a-kind emblems on various types of aircraft. The station letter-number system apparently was not used in Italy, but individual markings were common. Macchi flying boats operating from Porto Corsini were decorated with a "sharks-mouth" emblem which incorporated the Italian national roundel.

Occasionally, American flags were flown from aircraft. Probably the first such instance occurred during the "Veracruz Incident" in April/May of 1915, when the Curtiss AH-3, piloted by LTJG P.N.L. Bellinger, carried American Flags attached to its outboard inter-plane struts.

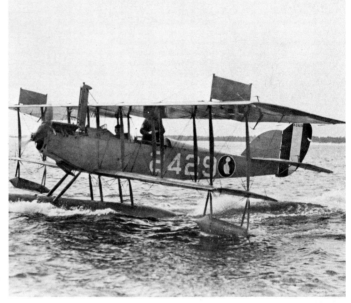

(Above) Burgess-built Curtiss N-9 at Pensacola in 1918. White serial number on fuselage, repeated in Black on White rudder stripe, was standard from mid-1917 into 1919. Insignia has been described as a "Dodo Bird" and was modified in later years. (USN via H.S. Gann)

Curtiss H-12, No. A-767, in standard WW I paint scheme. Last two digets of serial number appear on nose. Unique insignia shows mountain goat knocking the L out of KULTUR. (USN via H.S. Gann)

5

Modification of the standard Marine Corps "Globe and Anchor" was applied to aircraft of the Northern Bombing Group in late 1918. The Red, Blue and White cockade was the standard wing marking from mid-1917 into 1919. Officially, in 1922, the cockade in the insignia was replaced with the familiar Red and Yellow globe. In some instances "U.S. MARINES" appeared below the anchor with the Corps motto "Semper Fidelis" above the eagle. (USMC via C. Jansson)

On a public relations flight to New Orleans in 1919, Pensacola based Curtiss H-16, A-854, flew United States flags from rear interplane struts. (LCdr. J.W. Green)

At anchor, the aircraft displayed a commission pennant as well as the U.S. flags. Earliest display of flags in flight was probably at Vera Cruz, Mexico in 1914 when both the hydroaeroplane and the flying boat carried flags of the U.S. (LCdr. J.W. Green)

THE NINETEEN TWENTIES

Although Aluminum enamel was provided for in C&R Specification No. 4 of 30 March 1918, there is no evidence of it being actually authorized for use until June of 1919, when it was adopted as a replacement for Naval Gray on wings of new aircraft. It was not, however, to be applied over Gray or Khaki enamels. This change was made to reduce the temperature of fabric on aircraft and to lengthen it's service life, since low visibility was no longer critical. Metal parts were painted a Light Gray, while spar varnish was re-adopted as a finish for wooden interplane, pontoon, and landing gear struts.

As early as May of 1920, the Pacific Fleet Air Detachment at North Island, San Diego, reported its experiment with Yellow paint or enamel on the top surfaces of aircraft to increase visibility in the case of forced landings. Five years later, BuAer Technical Order No. 101 of 20 May 1925, required the use of Navy Yellow enamel on upper wings and the top surfaces of the stabilizer and elevators. There are indications that this only made official a practice that had gradually been adopted in service use.

The use of Bright (sometimes described as "Chrome") Yellow on the top wing surface was continued until February of 1941, when an overall Light Gray replaced the colorful "peacetime" Yellow. Yellow application to the top of the horizontal tail surfaces disappeared in the late twentys and early thirtys as solid colors or stripes on Aluminum finishes were adopted as a part of unit markings.

In order to insure maximum visibility, primary trainers were painted in an overall Bright Yellow and, regardless of type, were known as "Yellow Perils". In the early twentys, the Bureau serial number and the legend: "N.A.S. PENSACOLA" appeared on the fuselage side and, in some cases, on the vertical fin of aircraft utilized in training squadrons at Pensacola. Subsequently, large station numbers applied to the fuselage became standard.

Obsolete combat types served as advanced trainers at Pensacola, the only station giving a complete course of instruction, and sometimes retained the tail colors of the operational unit last assigned, until overhauled.

The Aluminum enamel on fabric surfaces gave an appearance of Silver and of Light Gray when applied to metal parts. As smooth-skin, semi-monocoque aircraft entered service in the early thirties, a much lighter shade of Gray was specified. A Silver finish was introduced in the mid-30's and retained until replaced by the overall Light Gray adopted as camouflage in early 1941.

Some aircraft retained their natural aluminum finish and those based at Anacostia often bore a "high polish" non-standard appearance as a result of buffing all aluminum surfaces.

All individual metallic fittings, except standard parts, such as bolts, nuts, washers, turnbuckles, etc., were marked with the manufacturer's piece number. Army-Navy standard parts were to be used whenever practicable and carried the designating A-N number.

All wing struts (including center section structs) were numbered to indicate their position on the airplane. The strut number was placed one-inch from the lower end of the strut and a corresponding number was placed on the lower wing or fuselage close to the lower wing strut fitting.

The front outermost strut, on the right, was numbered 1, and the remaining front struts were marked from right to left with consecutive odd numbers.

The right rear outermost strut was numbered 2, and the remaining rear struts were marked with consecutive even numbers. The numbers were applied in one-inch figures, originally in Insignia Blue paint; later in Black.

Each propeller blade was painted on both sides as follows:

> From tip to 4" from tip: Insignia Red
> 4" from tip to 8" from tip: Bright Yellow
> 8" from tip to 12" from tip: Insignia Blue
> 12" from tip to hub: Unfinished, except
>   that the Blue stripe could be extended an
>   additional 24" on the rear surface to reduce glare.

Piping systems, including filler caps and hand pulls, were identified by color codes applied in 1/2 inch bands "applied near each end and at such intermediate points as may be necessary to follow through the system."

A code of letters and figures was used to designate the doping system and date of application. The code was applied in one-inch letters, and placed on the underside of the fuselage, wings, and control panels. The code provided for a letter or letters to be assigned each finishing material, with the figures following to indicate the number of coats and date of completion. For example: ND2, PN3, 10-8-30, would mean: Nitrate Dope, two coats; Pigmented Nitrate Dope three coats; finished on 8 October 1930.

Lift points were identified by the words Lift Here in one-inch letters above the lift point. Handholes on lower wings, steps on floats, and wing walks were painted in Black. Manufacturers were responsible for most of the painting applied to aircraft, including the Marine Corps decalcomania, which was supplied by the Bureau of Aeronautics. Gradually, markings formally applied by operating units were painted on new aircraft before leaving the factory. Eventually, squadrons took delivery of new equipment in full markings, including unit insignia and pilot's name.

The 1917 star, and order of rudder stripes, were readopted in accordance with a directive dated 19 August 1919. Repainting was slow, however, and circles were still in evidence in the early 1920's. In describing the size of the star, painting directives stated that: "the diameter of the circumscribed circle be equal to the distance between the leading edge of the aileron and the leading edge of the wing, except that the diameter could not exceed five feet."

The star was to be positioned inboard from the wing tip a distance equal to the chord of the wing. Location of wing tip floats on floatplanes and amphibions resulted in repositioning of the star well inboard on the lower wing. In later years, the aircraft unit number was often applied outboard of the wing tip float.

From 1924 on, the Branch of Service marking — U.S. NAVY or U.S. MARINES — was applied to the fuselage or hull, replacing the Bureau Number. The size of the letters were "as large as the space permits, but in no case shall the height be less than eight inches". Later specifications directed that the letters be: "of an appropriate size so as to provide a neat appearance

Inconsistency in application of painting specifications is apparent in this April 1923 "incident" at Pensacola. (USN via H.S. Gann)

consistent with the space available and congruous with other markings applied''. Minimum height was set at four inches, with the last letter located approximately 12 inches from the rudder hinge.

From time to time, the Marine Corps carried the Branch of Service marking on the top wing. This appears to have been a perogative of command and was not standard throughout the Corps. The marking was utilized by VO-8M and VO-10M, equipped with Curtiss OC-2 aircraft in 1929-30; and by VO-7M (Curtiss O2C-2s) in 1933-34. The lettering usually followed the cranked-wing configuration of the aircraft and extended from star to star across the wing. Positioning of the lettering was such that it could be read by an overtaking aircraft.

Painting Specification SR-2 of 1 June 1931, called for application of the Branch of Service marking to the underside of the lower wings of Navy aircraft. The directive was modified to include the Marine Corps shortly afterwards. Approximately eight months later, however, the requirement was deleted. A limited number of aircraft, mostly those under construction at the time, received the application. Boeing F4B-3s of Fighting Squadron ONE, and Vought SU-1s of Scouting Squadron TWO, both attached to U.S.S. SARATOGA, are two examples. Most, but not all, of the Ford and Fokker transports carried the marking.

The ''U.S.'' of the legend was positioned on the right wing and ''NAVY'' or ''MARINES'' on the left. Several deviations from the standard, particularly in the case of transport aircraft, are confirmed by photographs. The legend appeared on the wing in such a position as to be read as the aircraft approached, and its use on transport types continued for several years.

With the application of the Branch of Service marking to the fuselage or hull, the Bureau Number was moved to the vertical fin. The ''A'' continued in use until 1930. Application was in three-inch letters painted in Blue or

Boeing F4B-3 (8898) of Fighting Squadron One-B (LCdr. F.P. Sherman) catches a wire aboard SARATOGA in March of 1932. Factory applied "U.S. NAVY" appears underwing in conformity with a short lived directive (less than one year). For a yet to be determined reason, neither VF-1B nor VF-3B applied section colors to the engine cowlings. Nose plates, however, were painted in accordance with specifications. (USN via H.S. Gann)

Black, except that White was specified on Red or Blue backgrounds. Deviations from the instructions were common practice, however.

Normally applied in horizontal alignment, the Bureau Number appeared in a vertical position in some instances. This was the case where the small fin area of the Boeing F3B-1 and the F4B series restricted horizontal application. Probably the most unusual application was on the Curtiss CT-1 of 1922, where the number (A-5890) appeared in large figures on the outboard sides of the twin floats.

In 1928, after a lapse of eleven years, the Model Designation reappeared. The fourth system to be utilized, it consisted of a combination of letters and numbers which identified the aircraft by type, manufacturer type sequence, and manufacturer code letter, and aircraft configuration sequence, Thus, the F8C-4 was a fighter aircraft, the eighth type, manufactured by Curtiss, and the fourth modification of the basic design.

The marking was usually applied in one line, centrally placed, in three inch letters, near the top of the rudder, on each side. Painting was White on the Blue and Red stripes, and Black on the White stripe in the case of aircraft not having colored tail surfaces. For aircraft with plain or colored tail surfaces, the Model Designation was applied in Black paint on White, Gray, Aluminum, Green or Yellow; and in White paint on Red or Blue. exceptions were common practice.

Normally, the name or trademark of the aircraft manufacturer was restricted to an identification plate, no larger than three inches by six inches, placed on the instrument board of each aircraft, conveying the following information:

    (a) Name, trademark, and address of aircraft manufacturer.
    (b) Manufacturers' model and serial number.
    (c) Navy model, class and serial number.
    (d) Date of delivery (approximate).

During the period 1925-1931, in many cases, the manufacturers' name was placed on both sides of the rudder; sometimes below and often above the Model Designation, as well as preceeding it. Variances in application were common. Infrequently, unofficial names, such as ''Hell Diver'' (Curtiss) and ''Corsair'' (Vought) were applied on factory painted aircraft delivered to operational units. Photographs confirm a few instances of company logos being applied to ''off the shelf'' and experimental aircraft.

UNIT MARKINGS
BACKGROUND

The "run-down" of naval aviation following World War I was such that activity was reduced almost to a "caretaker" status. Norfolk (Hampton Roads) on the East Coast, and San Diego (North Island) on the West, were the two main operational stations, with limited activity at several stations on the East Coast, Coco Solo in the Canal Zone, and Pearl Harbor, Hawaii.

Aircraft were assigned to a station, and were identified by side numbers or a letter-figure combination. Unit organization on a squadron basis began in 1920, and a year later, aircraft assigned to squadrons carried markings which identified them by class, squadron number, and aircraft number.

A reorganization of Naval Aviation resulted from a Chief of Naval Operations directive of 17 June 1922. Entitled: "Naval Aeronautic Organization for Fiscal Year 1923", existing units were redesignated, proposed units were identified, and long-range plans were described. This directive also established the system of numbering squadrons "...serially in each class in the order of the authorization for organizing them." It was so detailed as to specifically describe the unit identification of each aircraft in every unit.

The numbering system consisted of a three-character group in which the first figure was the number of the squadron, followed by a letter identifying the class. The third character was the number of the aircraft within the squadron. Close observance of this policy through the ensuing years resulted in unit redesignations simply to maintain numerical continuity. This, coupled with redesignations due to change in class, transfers between carriers, and battleship and cruiser divisional switches, were confusing at the time, and present a formidable challange to the historian of today. The reaction of Naval aviation personnel to the procedure is reflected in the May, 1938 issue of the Naval Institute PROCEEDINGS, in which Lieutenant Ben Scott Custer suggested assigning the name of an American Indian tribe to each squadron in order to maintain its identity.

The three-plane section was the basic unit in squadron organization, with the standard complement of a carrier squadron established at 18 aircraft, formed in two divisions of three sections each. Budgetary limitations resulted in under-strength units into the mid-30s, particularly in the Marine Corps. Standard carrier organization consisted of an air group of four squadrons: Fighting, Bombing, Scouting and Torpedo. Due to space limitations, RANGER and WASP did not carry a torpedo squadron. These two air groups eventually consisted of two Fighting and two Scouting squadrons. Each Air Group was identified by its carrier's name (i.e., SARATOGA Air Group) and it was not until mid-1942 that air groups were identified simply by number. The billet of Air Group Commander was not authorized until 1938.

Each Fighting squadron was assigned one scouting-type aircraft, which flew with the squadron to perform liaison/communication functions. In addition, one or two obsolescent observation or scouting types were attached for target towing and instrument training purposes. These aircraft did not accompany the squadron aboard the carrier, nor did the two or three aircraft assigned to the Carrier Division flag officer.

The shore-based Torpedo units of the 1920's, and their Patrol squadron

successors, operated six, nine or twelve aircraft in the usual three-plane sections. For many years, the Tables of Organization showed these units assigned to seaplane tenders (i.e., AROOSTOOK, WRIGHT, etc.). In actual practice, the squadrons operated from shore stations except for relatively short periods of deployment with a tender.

Battleship-based aviation experienced a number of organizational changes before the three-plane section became standard. As catapults were placed aboard in the early 1920s, one or two VE-7, later UO-1 type observation aircraft, were assigned to each ship. At one time, it was planned that a battleship aviation unit would consist of one fighting, one observation, and one utility type aircraft.

Fighting Squadron ONE operated its TS-1s on twin floats from battleships in 1925, and Fighting Squadron TWO's single-float FU-1s were aboard battleships in 1928. The Bureau of Aeronautics Weekly News Letter of 11 January 1928, stated: "The squadron numbers of VF-2B have been changed to correspond with the squadron numbers of the VO planes on the various ships; such as 2-F-10 would be with 1/10 or 2-F-11 to be paired with 1/11, etc."

While there is no further record of fighting types operating regularly from battleships three-place Loening OL-type amphibions were assigned to most battleships for a period of time in the late 1920s. By 1930, three-plane sections of Vought O2U-or-O3U-type observation planes was standard, with the squadron number matching the number of the battleship division. Observation Squadron ONE was aboard ships of Battleship Division ONE, for example, with the first section of each squadron aboard the division flagship.

Cruiser-based squadrons deviated from the standard three-plane section. Lack of deck space limited the ten Omaha-class "scout" cruisers to a section of two aircraft. The larger "treaty" cruisers, with amidship hanger space, operated four-plane sections. Subsequent cruiser construction placed the catapults at the stern with below-deck hangar space. Therefore, regardless of size, the color assigned to sections remained constant. However, the numbers of the aircraft within sections varied in relation to the size of the section.

Utility squadrons operated a varying number of aircraft of different types. Fleet-attached squadrons (VJ-1 and VJ-2) usually observed the three-plane section organization. Those assigned to the Shore Establishment (Naval Districts) usually numbered their aircraft in numerical sequence. Although listed as squadrons under the Shore Establishment, and assigned Naval District numbers, the Training Squadrons at Pensacola (ONE through FIVE)

Typical of the battleship-based aircraft of the mid-1920's Vought UO-1, No. A-6607, as it was delivered to NAS San Diego in January of 1924 for assignment to the USS TENNESSEE BB-43. Before being stricken in April of 1927, the aircraft was assigned to WEST VIRGINIA BB-48, MARYLAND BB-46, NEW YORK BB-34 and NEW MEXICO BB-40. The aircraft also was assigned to VF-2B and VS-2B. (USN via H.S. Gann)

were actually station-based aircraft. This was also true of the Training squadrons giving preliminary training at Great Lakes, Norfolk, and San Diego. Reserve units were organized as squadrons and generally observed regular Navy practice in markings of their aircraft. Marine Corps Reserve units used the same aircraft as the Navy units, however, the assigned aircraft carried Navy squadron designations.

In 1922, changes to administrative procedures in the Navy resulted in an extensive revision to correspondence and filing practices. One effect on naval aviation was to assign the letter "V" (for heavier-than-air) to precede the class letter of a squadron. For example, Fighting Squadron ONE was identified as VF Squadron ONE (short title VF-1). Suffix letters to indicate Fleet or Force assignments were adopted on 1 July 1927. These were:

A for Asiatic Fleet	M for Marine Corps
B for Battle Force	R for Reserve
F for Base Force	S for Scouting Fleet

Fighting Squadron ONE was now identified as VF Squadron ONE-B (short title: VF-1B). The letter "Z" identified lighter-than-air activity.

These prefix and suffix letters were not to be painted on aircraft. However, exceptions were numerous. Suffix letters were dropped by carrier squadrons in the extensive reorganization of 1 July 1937, when the four squadrons of each air group were renumbered to conform to the hull number of the parent carrier. With the exception of VF-2B (LEXINGTON), all carrier squadrons were renumbered. There was one change in class (VB-1B became VT-2) and six squadrons were in the process of receiving new equipment.

Berlinger-Joyce OJ-2s were assigned only to light cruiser squadrons, organized in two plane sections. Leader of the third section of VS-5B, assigned to Cruiser Division Two, No. 9409 carries Blue cowl, fuselage band, wing chevron and tail band. First section was aboard USS TRENTON CL-11, and the second section aboard the USS MARBLEHEAD CL-12. The squadron omitted "dashes" between figures of the side number. Oversize "U.S. NAVY" with ship name below was non-standard. (Ed McCollum)

Fleet Squadron Re-Organization
1 July 1937

Suffix letters were abandoned by battleship, cruiser, and patrol squadrons at the same time.

The eight cruiser-based scouting squadrons were redesignated in mid-1937, becoming cruiser-scouting (VCS) and were renumberd to conform to their parent cruiser divisions. The four battleship-based observations squadrons (VO) were not affected, having matched numbers with their battleship divisions in the late 1920s.

Patrol squadrons continued to be numbered sequentially (although skipping the unlucky "13") until 1939 when the new Patrol Wing organization became effective. Now, the first digit in a patrol squadron number indicated the Wing and the second digit the squadron within the Wing. Thus, VP-7 became VP-11 of Patrol Wing ONE.

1939 PATROL SQUADRON RE-ORGANIZATION *

INSIGNIA	OLD NUMBER	NEW NUMBER
Great White Albatross	VP-7	VP-11
Goose Flying Under the Sun	VP-9	VP-12
———		VP-13**
Sitka Spruce Tree	VP-21	VP-14
Elephant Standing on Cloud	VP-1	VP-21
Griffin and Numeral 4	VP-4	VP-22
Pegasus in Circle	VP-6	VP-23
Winged 8-Ball	VP-8	VP-24
Bomb in Compass Rose	VP-10	VP-25
Wings Over the Globe	VP-18	VP-26
Keystone Cop	VP-2	VP-31
Standing Elephant with Spyglass	VP-3	VP-32
Wings Over Panama	VP-5	VP-33
Husky Dog	VP-16	VP-41
Seal Balancing Bomb on Nose	VP-17	VP-42
Polar Bear on Mountain	VP-19	VP-43
Mine in Horseshoe	VP-20	VP-44
———		VP-45**
Totem Pole and Mt. Rainier	VP-12	VP-51
Six Geese in Flight	VP-14	VP-52
Indian Scout Kneeling	VP-15	VP-53
Head of Odin	VP-11	VP-54

*W.T. Larkings "US Navy Aircraft 1921-1941."   **Operated in late 1939 only, both were new units.

UNIT MARKINGS
Side Numbers

In what appears to be the first use of unit identification Loening M-8O's of the Air Detachment, Pacific Fleet (North Island), carried a large letter-number figure, such as "P-2" on each side of the fuselage. At the same time (1919-20), a unit of F-5-L flying boats, operating on the East Coast used the last two digits of the aircraft's Bureau Number as side number identification. These were applied to each side of the hull, midway between wings and tail. A year later, having re-equipped with overhauled aircraft, sequentially-assigned numbers were adopted. The Torpedo unit, operating NAF PT-1s and 2s, used sequentially assigned numbers.

With the transfer of the U.S. Fleet to the Pacific, the gradual expansion of the aeronautical organization was centered at North Island. Spotting Squadrons, operating DH-4B aircraft, were formed to provide "fall-of-shot" service to battleships. Combat Squadrons, equipped with VE-7 aircraft, were formed for defense of the fleet, while long range scouting was the mission of the Seaplane Patrol Squadron.

On the East Coast, two Scouting Squadrons (later merged into one) and one Torpedo Squadron, operated from Norfolk (Hampton Roads) and the air stations still in use on the Atlantic Coast. Each F-5-L was painted in an individual camouflage scheme, while the PT twin-float seaplanes used the standard finish, but with individual insignia on the fuselage forward of the squadron number.

When the reorganization of 1922 became effective, seven squadrons, two on the East Coast and five at North Island, were in commission. Unit designations and typical side numbers were:

Prior To Reorganization

H.R. Scouting Squadron-1	1-S-1
H.R. Torpedo Pllane Sdn-1	1-T-1
S.D. Spotting Squadron-3	S-301
S.D. Spotting Squadron-4	S-401
S.D. Combat Squadron-3	C-301
S.D. Combat Squadron-4	C-401
S.D. Seaplane Patrol Sqdn-1	1

Effective 1, July 1922

Scounting Squadron One	(VS-1)	1-S-1
Torp & Bomb Sqdn One	(VT-1)	1-T-1
Observation Sqdn Two	(VO-2)	2-1
Observation Sqdn One	(VO-1)	1/1
Fighting Squadron Two	(VF-2)	2F1
Fighting Squadron One	(VF-1)	1F1
Torp & Bomb Sqdn Two	(VT-2)	2T1

Marine Corps units at the same time were:

Fighting Squadron-1	Quantico
Observation Squadron-3	Quantico
Observation Squadron-2	Haiti
Scouting Squadron-1	Guam
Observation Squadron-1	Haiti

Curtiss/NAF F-5L aircraft of the East Coast Scouting Squadron in the early 1920s carried individual camouflage paint schemes. The last two digits of the aircraft's serial number appeared as the plane number. Later, the squadron's aircraft were numbered sequentially. (via W.A. Riley)

Sparkling DH-4B from Spotting Squadron Four displays the four-star flag of Secretary of the Navy Denby, one of the largest flags to be flown from a Navy aircraft. NAS San Diego in 1921 in front of the LTA hangar. (USN via W.A. Riley)

DH-4B aircraft of Spotting Squadron Four at North Island in 1921. Vought VE-7s of Combat Squadrons Three and Four complete the line up. (USN via W. A. Riley)

UNIT MARKINGS
Presentation

The three character group, often described as the "side number", was carried by all aircraft assigned to squadrons. The characters were as large as permissible and were separated by a dash (-). They were applied to each side of the fuselage, on top of the upper wing, and on both sides of the lower wing.

In the case of flying boats, side positioning was forward of the wings. For all other aircraft, the first character (squadron number) was located in line with the cockpit; "of an appropriate size" ahead of the Branch of Service marking, "in such position that the centers of the two groups are on a horizontal axial plane." Marine Corps aircraft seldom carried the top and lower wing application which was abandoned by the Navy about 1929.

The ten class letters assigned were as follows:

B	- Bombing	/	- Observation
F	- Fighting	P	- Patrol
J	- Utility	S	- Scouting
M	- Miscellaneous	T	- Torpedo
N	- Training	X	- Experimental

DH-4B aircraft of Observation Squadron Two, formerly Spotting Squadron Three, over San Diego in 1922. White cowls with the aircraft number repeated on a White band across the front of the radiator. 2-9 displays a White "E", one of the earliest applications to appear on a Navy airplane. (USN via Silver Eagles Association Collection)

The slash (/) was adopted for Observation on the assumption that "O" might be confused with zero. The slash was dropped in 1930 and replaced by "O". In applying the side numbers to Marine Corps aircraft, the class letter was reduced in size and placed within a circle of the same size as the other figures. However, the dash (-) was usually omitted until the extensive renumbering of 1937 which saw the Marine Corps conforming to Navy procedures. In some instances, a small "M" (for Marines) was placed slightly below and to the rear of the circle enclosing the class letter.

During Fiscal Year 1928, LEXINGTON was assigned to the Scouting Force and a small "s" was applied below and to the rear of the class letter of the three squadrons in the air group (VF-3s, VF-5s, and VT-1s). Only three weeks old, VT-3s, originally planned as the second Torpedo unit for LEXINGTON, became (on 9-30-27) VT-9S. Based at Hampton Roads, as part of the Scouting Force, the small "s" was applied as described above. Some, but not all, of the remaining shore-based squadrons assigned to the Scouting Force, (VJ-2s and various Patrol Squadrons), also used the small "s".

Painting specifications described the side number identification to be used for squadrons assigned to Naval Air Stations, including those assigned to a specific mission. Two letters representing the abbreviated name of the station and the sequential plane number, separated by a dash, comprised the side number. If the station name was one word, the first and last letters were used; if two words, the first letter in each word; (i.e., "HR-10" for tenth plane at Hampton Roads.)

For squadrons assigned a mission, the appropriate class letter was placed between the station letters and the plane number.

Aircraft assigned to Naval Air Stations (non-squadron) testing facilities, etc., carried the appropriate name as a side number. Examples of this identification are:

N.A.S.	ANACOSTIA	Naval Air Station, Anacostia, D.C.
N.P.G.	DAHLGREN	Naval Proving Grounds, Dahlgren, VA
N.A.F.		Naval Aircraft Factory, Philadelphia
I.N.A.	(Location)	Inspector of Naval Aircraft
GINA	(Location)	Genl. Inspt. of Naval Aircraft (rare)

Size of the letters approximated that of squadron side numbers, with considerable variation apparent from a study of photographs. The periods following letters were frequently omitted. Top and under wing application was seldom employed.

In the mid-1920s, most shore-based squadrons (Utility, Patrol, and Torpedo) carried side numbers which were an abbreviation of their official disignation. For example: Torpedo Squadron EIGHT, operating from Coco Solo, under the jurisdiction of the Fifteenth Naval District, was listed as VT-8D-15, with side numbers appearing as 8-T-1. However, Utility Squadron THREE, operating from San Diego (Eleventh Naval District) applied its offical designation, VJ-D11-3 to a Vought VE-9. In the mid-1930s, having been redesignated VJ-D11-5, abbreviated side numbers were used. Concurrently, at Norfolk, (formerly Hampton Roads), the station squadron carried side numbers as: 4-M-1, for the seldom used Miscellaneous class.

At first, painting specifications called for application of side numbers in True Blue paint. This was later changed to Black, and as fuselage bands came into use, White was used where necessary for contrast, such as a class letter on a Red or Blue band. In order to maintain a uniform appearance, the dashes separating figures were sometimes half Black, (outside the band) and half White (on the band).

Rare application of dual series of side numbers. Newly acquired Boeing F3B-1's of Light Bombing Squadron One-B (ex-VF-5B) carry standard marking while Curtiss F6C-3's (original equipment) are marked: 1-B-A, 1-B-B, 1-B-C, etc. (via H.S. Gann)

Late 1922 photo of Lt. Ben H. Wyatt, center, and unidentified Chief Aviation Pilot and civilian, in front of DH-4B of Observation Squadron One (1/1) used in "Around the United States" flight. VO-1 used a slash (/) and VO-2 a dash (-) between squadron number and aircraft number. (USN via San Diego Aerospace Museum)

Vought O2U-4 (A-8316) of USS SALT LAKE CITY CA-25 in January of 1929. Scouting Squadron Six-S was a light cruiser squadron. SLC was apparently assigned pending completion of PENSACOLA CA-24 and other heavy cruisers. Strict adherence to painting specifications is apparent in the application of "Vought O2U-4" across the rudder stripes in contrasting paint. Lack of "dashes" between side numbers and use of "U.S.S." indicates non-conformity. (USN via S. Norris)

Boeing FB-1s of Marine Fighting Squadron One. Circle around mission letter identified Marine Corps units. Data legend below cockpit was unique to Marines. Large "Globe and Anchor" was typical of the period (1926). (USN via W.A. Riley)

Vought O2U-1 on catapult of USS IDAHO BB-42 in 1929 as ship turns to bring wind across stern. Tail color is unknown. Application of ship name below rear cockpit was typical of the late 1920s and early 1930s. Nose plate appears to be unpainted. (USN via H.S. Gann)

(Above) Loening OL-8A, (A-8032) with side number of 2-P-1. Unusual assignment of an amphibian to a patrol squadron (VP-2S) in 1929. Application of "LOENING OL-8A" in Black and White paint across rudder stripes is in accordance with painting specifications. (USN via S. Norris)

Official reports and other sources (circa 1928-1934) make reference to a "Wing" organization, and although no formal structure is shown in tables of organization, during the summer fleet concentration at San Diego, squadrons were grouped by type for certain activities. During parades or "fly bys" each "Wing" was led by the senior squadron commander. These Curtiss O2C-2 and F8C-4 aircraft bearing the legend "FIGHTING WING" indicates that at least a temporary organization was established on occasion. (via D. Carter)

(Above) Martin T3M-2 of VT-8D-15, based at Fleet Air Base, Coco Solo, 1928. Wing legend is 8-CS-T-4, with side number abbreviated as 8-T-4. Lack of national insignia on upper wing is unusual. White after-body of floats and Black highlighted rudder hinge is noteworthy. (via F. C. Dickey)

During a three year tour at NAS San Diego, Consolidated NY-1 (A-7197) was assigned to the air station, VO-8M and VN 7-D-11. Lack of underwing national insignia and "bomb" insignia are noteworthy. (via Silver Eagles Association Collection)

(Below) Curtiss TS-1, No. 6308, of Fighting Squadron One with reversed presentation of number (1-F-21) on undersurface of lower right wing. Lack of national insignia was not uncommon in the 1920s. (USN via San Diego Aerospace Museum)

UNIT MARKINGS
Color Code

The use of distinguishing colors to identify squadrons and sections within squadrons began about 1925. The practice was initiated by the squadrons, and was not directed by higher authority. The TS-1 aircraft of VF-1 were painted in various colors, by section, with the first section using Black. Red, Light Blue, Yellow, not necessarily in that order, were also used, and one section was not painted. Section leaders carried a fuselage band matching the tail color. Photographic evidence indicates the VF-2 painted its F6C aircraft in a similar fashion.

Results of the use of color were reported to the Bureau of Aeronautics by Commander, Aircraft Squadrons, Battle Force, in a letter dated 1 June 1927: "All planes of the Battle Fleet have been painted with distinguishing marks as follows: squadrons have been divided into tactical groups, or sections, and the tail surfaces of each group were painted the same color for purposes of identification. The leader of each group has had a band of the same color painted around the fuselage. The colors used have been Red, Yellow, Light Blue and Black. All have been satisfactory except the Black, which has been difficult to maintain in a neat appearance. During this present summer concentration, Green will be substituted for the Black."

About the same time, squadrons began applying a single-color to the tail surfaces of their aircraft. Photographs of VF-1 in formation, circa 1926, indicate that the tail surfaces of it's TS-1 planes were all painted the same color, probably Red. At the 1927 National Air Races in Spokane, Washington, VF-1B, now with Boeing FB-5 aircraft, carried Red tails. VF-B (ex VF-2), also with FB-5's, had White tail surfaces. Photographic evidence confirms that fuselage bands had not been standardized. In early 1928, VF-2B (newly organized in January of 1927), painted the vertical fin of its Vought FU-1 aircraft a Dark Blue, but retained rudder stripes. Photographs of 2-F-4, indicates that the section leader band was White.

In May of 1928, VT-2B adopted Red as its tail color. However, fuselage bands differed from the standard, later to be promulgated in painting specification SR-2, dated 1 June 1931. Leaders of the first and second sections carried dark color fuselage bands, while the band on 2-T-7, leader of the third section was White.

By early 1929, almost all Navy squadrons had adopted a solid or broad stripe tail color and standardization in the order of section colors had been achieved. The time lag between procedures in effect in the operating forces and the issuance of official directives is confirmed by a Bureau of Aeronautics letter dated 10 December 1930, as follows: All markings used to

(Below) Curtiss F6C-1 (A-6969) of "new" Fighting Squadron Two, displays unique "meat ball" circles inboard of national insignia, probably a forerunner of chevron markings. This Squadron adopted Blue as a tail color, although it may not have been applied to aircraft at this time. (1927). (USN via H.S. Gann)

(Above) Curtiss F6C-1 (later-2) of Fighting Squadron Two in 1926. At this time, section colors were in effect, but were soon replaced by tail colors assigned to squadrons; VF-2 adopted White. (USN via W.A. Riley)

(Below) Vought UO-1 (A-6859) with side number of 3-S-7. Aircraft was interim equipment for newly-formed Scouting Squadron Two-B in mid-1928. Fin and rudder have been overpainted (probably Yellow). (USN via H.S. Gann)

designate squadrons or sections shall (emphasis supplied) conform to the following colors:

1st section or the lowest numbered squadron	Insignia Red
2nd section or 2nd lowest numbered squadron	White
3rd section or 3rd lowest numbered squadron	Insignia Blue
4th section or 4th lowest numbered squadron	Black
5th section or 5th lowest numbered squadron	Green
6th section or 6th lowest numbered squadron	Lemon Yellow

A number of factors precluded the assignment of tail colors to squadrons as directed in the letter. Current usage, renumbering moves between carriers, units operating similar or identical types, tradition and perogative of command were all involved.

A serious identification problem arose when RANGER's four squadrons joined the air groups of LEXINGTON and SARATOGA at North Island in April of 1935. These twelve squadrons, plus the two LANGLEY-assigned units newly comissioned on 1 July 1935, reflected a variety of tail colors as follows:

CARRIER	HULL NO.	Squadron	A/C	TAIL COLOR
LANGLEY	CV-1	VF-1B	F4B-4	Red
		VS-4B	O3U-1	Red
LEXINGTON	CV-2	VF-2B	F2F-1	Yellow
		VF-5B	FF-1	Blue
		VS-3B	SF-1	Yellow
		VB-1B	BM-1/2	Yellow
SARATOGA	CV-3	VF-6B	F4B-4	White
		VS-2B	SU-2/3	White
		VB-2B	BFC-2	Red
		VT-2B	TG-2	Red
RANGER	CV-4	VF-3B	F2F-1	Green
		VB-3B	BG-1	Green
		VB-5B	BG-1	Green
		VS-1B	SU-4	Green

Resolution of the problem was directed by Commander, Aircraft, Battle Force in an 22 October 1935 letter, addressed to Fleet Units and the Bureau of Aeronautics, which stated, in part: "Due to the large number of squadrons now attached to Aircraft Battle Force, it is impractical to continue the policy of assigning tail colors that permit the identification of squadrons within a carrier group. The future policy will be to assign the same color to each group of carrier squadrons."

(Below) Fighting Squadron Two-B served aboard battleships in 1928. CPO insignia was applied to the fin (probably Blue) with "Vought FU-1" in White across the rudder stripes. (USN via San Diego Aerospace Museum)

(Below) North Island in May of 1932. Scouting Squadron Two-B stands by for inspection. Vought O3U-2s (soon to be redesignated SU-1s) carry full markings, but lack "Pointer Dog" insignia. Pilot and three-man crews await inspection party (posing for camera in front of 2-S-5). A SARATOGA Loening OL-9 completes the group. (USN via R.P. Gill)

(Above) T3M-2s of Torpedo Squadron Two-B (SARATOGA) at San Diego in 1928. Effeciency pennant in fuselage band was non-standard. 2-T-10 was the leader of the fourth section, Black band is carried, but apparently no wing chevron. Red tail. (USN via H.S. Gann)

17

Martin T3M-2s of VP-2S (second section) show rare application of secton colors to cowlings of water cooled engined aircraft. Slant-edged dashes in side numbers were used when squadron was VT-3-D-15. Solid Red tail color was continued onto the after fuselage. Color of nose section appears to match that of twin floats; the color was probably unique to Coco Solo based units. (USN via F.C. Dickey)

"The tail colors will be allocated as follows:

SARATOGA	(White)
LEXINGTON	(Yellow)
RANGER	(Green)
LANGLEY	(Red)
ENTERPRISE*	(Blue)
YORKTOWN*	(Black)

New or overhauled aircraft should be so painted before delivery. Airplanes will retain their present tail color until turned in for overhaul." However, it appears that repainting was mostly accomplished at the squadron level prior to overhaul.

Several squadrons reported repainting problems, as noted from a Bureau of Aeronautics News Letter of the time. VB-2B said that Red tended to predominate when over-sprayed with White. Two coats of White enamel were recommended. VT-2B's solution was to utilize a mixture of shellac, Aluminum dope and Blue lacquer as a sealer. This prevented the Red from showing through the White as "an effininate Pink". VB-1B reported stripping some planes during overhaul and overpainting others, Green or Yellow, as a result of it's late-1935 transfer from LEXINGTON to RANGER.

Progress of the repainting program was reported by the type Commander to C-in-C, U.S. Fleet (CINCUS) that the changes in squadron tail colors would be completed by 1 February 1936.

The one-color-per-carrier painting scheme was confirmed by the Bureau of

*When commissioned.

Aeronautics in a May 1936 letter to N.A.S., Pensacola, in answering a request for information for use in teaching cadets. It would appear, then, that the change to tail color by a carrier air group preceeded the change to unit designation by carrier hull number by approximately six months.

Her usefullness as an aircraft carrier at an end, LANGLEY was redesignated as a Seaplane Tender in September of 1936. Reassignment of her two squadrons; VF-1B to LEXINGTON and VS-4B to SARATOGA, would call for a change in tail colors to conform to policy. It can only be assumed that repainting occurred, indications are that it did take place, however.

LANGLEY's redesignation did not affect carrier air group tail colors, however. Amendment No. 1 to SR-2a, dated 15 March 1937, affirmed the policy of one-color-per-carrier, and assigned LANGLEY's Red to YORKTOWN. WASP, due to commission in early 1940, received Black.

During April, May and June of 1937, while organizing at Norfolk, YORKTOWN and ENTERPRISE squadrons carried "paper" designations with -7B and -8B numbers. These were presumably assigned for administrative purposes, inasmuch as only a few obsolescent aircraft were on hand. Exceptions were the two Fighting squadrons, VF-1B and VF-3B, soon to become VF-6 and VF-5, respectively, which were "decommissioned" on the west coast.

Actually, except for routine end-of-the-year re-assignments, most of the personnel took leave and reassembled at Norfolk. Aircraft of both squadrons, Boeing F4B-4s of VF-1B and Grumman F2F-1s of VF-3B, were ferried cross-country and delivered to the "new" units at Norfolk. Repainting of tail surfaces to conform to the new carrier assignments was accomplished as well as new side numbers to reflect the appropriate group number. VF-3B, now VF-5, retained its "Striking Eagle" insignia, while VF-1B, now VF-6, adopted a "Shooting Star".

General Aviation PJ-1 in paint scheme utilized by Coast Guard aircraft from 1926 to 1936. FLB-54 (Flying Life Boat) appears on vertical fin. The five PJ-1s, acquired in 1932, were assigned "star" names which were applied on the bow, forward of the cockpit. FLB-54 was ACAMAR. (USCG via T.E. Doll)

Altough obviously in use prior to the issuance of specification SR-2, section colors were then officially prescribed as follows:

- Royal Red	1st Section
- White	2nd Section
- True Blue	3rd Section
- Black	4th Section
- Willow Green	5th Section
- Lemon Yellow	6th Section

The directive further stated that the use of fuselage bands, wing chevrons, and nose cowl painting was to "facilitate maneuvers and rendezvous". The minor conflict in terminology (Insignia Red vs Royal Red.) was resolved in favor of Insignia Red.

Almost without exception, the naval aeronautic organization closely observed the six colors prescribed for section markings. A 20-inch wide band was painted around the fuselage (from top of sponson to top of sponson in the case of flying boats) of each section leader. In some instances, the band was placed forward or aft of the side number. Standard application was to position the band across the class letter, and all or part of the dashes between the squadron number and the plane number. The band was often outlined in Black or White, while the class letter and the dashes were painted to provide contrast.

Specification SR-2 was permissive (using "may") in prescribing the use of fuselage bands, while SR-2a, dated 1 February 1933 was mandatory (using "shall") in its terminology.

Section colors were applied to the cowlings of liquid-cooled engines and to the nose plates of air-cooled engines. Specification SR-2 stated that: "a band 12 inches wide, beginning at the nose on water-cooled planes, shall be painted in the colors conforming to those designated for each section". Relatively few liquid-cooled engines were in squadron service when cowl painting became standard.

The nose plates of air-cooled engines were painted as follows: Section leader: completely; No. 2 plane: upper half; and No. 3 plane: lower half. The entire width of anti-drag rings was painted, with the break between color and

Third section leader of four plane unit based aboard USS NEW ORLEANS CA-32. Ship name below side number is typical of heavy cruiser squadrons in the mid-1930s. Careful attention to painting specifications is apparent in the contrasting colors on the side number and the ship's name. (Ed McCollum)

Douglas RD-2 in "all aluminum" paint scheme adopted in 1936. Top wing surface was Chrome Yellow with no national markings, however, "U.S.C.G." appeared for some time on various aircraft. Assigned name ADHARA appears on bow. (USCG via T.E. Doll)

Vought O3U-1 at Norfolk in 1936. Red tailed "Corsair" from three plane section aboard USS OKLAHOMA BB-37. Co-author William A. Riley flew in rear cockpit of this aircraft on many occasions. His flight log shows aircraft Bu.No to be 8553. (W.A. Riley)

Squadron leader of Observation Squadron One-B at Naval Reserve Air Base, Long Beach in 1935 or 1936. First section was aboad USS TEXAS BB-35, second on the USS NEW YORK BB-34, third on USS OKLAHOMA BB-37. Tail color is Red. "Dashes" in contrasting Black and White paint are noteworthy. (Ed McCollum)

White tailed Boeing F4B-4 (No. 9026) of VF-6B at NRAB, Long Beach in 1935. Fuselage band and standard wing chevron in Black are outlined in White. "Dashes" between figures of the side number are totally within the band. (Ed McCollum).

Vought SU-2s of VO-8M, 1933. Circled / can just barely be seen on the upper wing. Vertical stabilizer mounted "Ace of Spades" insignia. Red/White and Blue vertical stripes are carried on the tail. (USMC via John Caler)

Gray paint (on other than section leaders) often outlined in Black or White. On full cowlings, the width of the paint was limited to 18 inches and often outlined in Black or White, as appropriate.

In an apparent perogative of command, for a period of time, in 1932-33, neither VF-1B (F4B-3s) nor VF-3B (F4B-4s) painted the anti-drag rings of their Boeing fighters. Nose plates, however, were painted in the usual manner.

At first, the fourth plane in the four-plane sections of cruiser-based VS (VCS after 7-1-37) squadrons carried an unpainted cowl. From about 1936, when SOC type planes were on hand, a 12 inch wide stripe was painted on the top and on the bottom of the engine cowling.

Wing chevrons, corresponding to the section color were painted on the top wing of all planes in the section. The plane number was painted in the center of the chevron "in figures of the largest practicable size". Painting specifications directed that the chevron point forward, however, SR-2 stated: "When a wing shape is such that the specified chevron does not allow sufficient area for the number, either parallel bands or a chevron pointing aft may be substituted". Center section cut-outs in the top wings of many bi-plane types restricted the size of the chevron and the space for applying the plane number; therefore, reversed positioning was common practice.

Another reason for using reversed chevrons appears in the Bureau of Aeronautics News Letter of 1 May 1936. Scouting Squadron TWO, transitioning from SU-2/3 to SBU-1 equipment at the time stated: "The experience of the older pilots in VS-2 brought forth a general consensus of opinion that the inverted chevron is by far the most desirable for position keeping in formation work. In this case the point of the chevron is over the pilot's head, even in cases where the upper wing panel is shaped so as to give the pilot an unobstructed overhead view, in which event the chevron is broken, but its legs are still 45 degrees from the pilot's head forward. It is generally concurred in that the chevron, with peak forward, is decorative but scarcely useful, inasmuch as the pilot must construct an imaginary line through the pilots head parallel to the leg of the existing chevron; this is exeptionally difficult when executing a turn, as the horizontal perspective is destroyed, whereas the inverted chevron permits accurate execution of the turn."

Photographs confirm a few instances in which "solid" wing chevrons, more accurately described as triangles, were used. All planes in VT-1B carried "solid" chevrons on T4M-/ aircraft, circa 1929. At the time of its

Fleet Patrol Wing Markings
Per SR2B

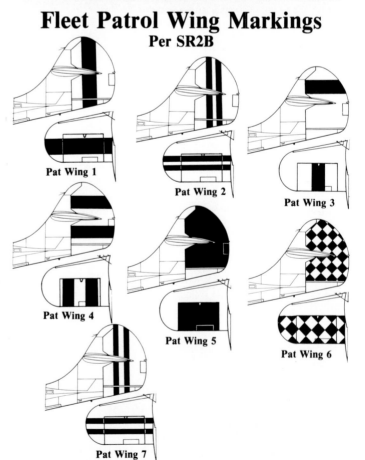

Pat Wing 1

Pat Wing 2

Pat Wing 3

Pat Wing 4

Pat Wing 5

Pat Wing 6

Pat Wing 7

First plane of four plane section onboard the USS MINNEAPOLIS CA-36 in 1936. Wing chevron, cowling and fuselage band are Insignia White, while tail bands are Black. Leading edge of the bottom wing is Orange-Yellow while individual aircraft number inside wing chevron is Insignia White. SOC-1 is with VS-12S and carries side legend 12-S-5 with ship name painted under fuselage codes. (USN/National Archives).

Second plane of four plane section from MINNEAPOLIS. Top half of cowling painted Insignia White, no fuselage band. Side coding is 12-S-6. Once again the leading edge of bottom wing is painted with Orange-Yellow paint. (USN/National Archives).

Third plane from MINNEAPOLIS four plane section. 12-S-7 has lower half of cowling painted Insignia White. Leading edge of lower wing painted the same as 12-S-5 and 12-S-6. (USN/National Archives)

Fourth plane of four plane section from MINNEAPOLIS. Fourth aircraft in group featured top and bottom cowl stripes in appropriate color. 12-S-8 also has leading edge of lower wing painted Orange-Yellow. Top surface of top wing is glossy Orange-Yellow. Metal parts of plane painted Light Grey, while fabric covered parts are painted with Aluminum lacquer. (USN/National Archives).

record-breaking, long distance flights in 1931, VP-19F, operating P2Y-1 aircraft, applied "solid" chevrons to section leader aircraft (10-P-1 and 10-P-4) only. A squadron pilot stated the marking "facilitated formation flying".

As low-wing monoplane equipment came into service in late 1937, it became necessary to split the chevron, with one half applied to each wing. Placement of the plane number was either inboard or outboard of the chevron half stripe. Specification SR-2B of 8 October 1940 formalized this application by stating: "For low-wing monoplanes and for patrol planes, the plane number shall be painted on each side of the wing panel, midway between the star insignia and the extremity of the center wing panel. On patrol planes, the number shall also be painted on the lower surface of the wing, legible from the rear, and a lower altitude".

The Marine Corps observed Navy marking directves only in general terms until the redesignation/renumbering of 1 July 1937. The dashes in side numbers were often omitted when painting on fuselage bands and wing chevrons. Tail surface painting ranged from rudder stripes to solid colors to distinctive designs.

In the mid-1930s, the "Acey-Duecy" markings of VO-6M were obviously inspired by the playing board of the Navy/Marine Corps version of the ancient game of Backgammon. VO-7M's Red-White-Blue markings were equally as colorful. These two units were operating Curtiss O2C-1 aircraft at the time.

Martin T4M-1s of Torpedo Squadron One-B display solid chevrons and side number repeated on upper wing. 1-T-7 is unmarked. Lack of national insignia on upper wing is noteworthy. (USN via W.A. Riley)

Consolidated P2Y-1 of Patrol Squadron Ten enroute from San Diego to San Francico with Adm. D.F. Sellers on board, January of 1934, just prior to flight to Hawaii. 10-P-1 and 10-P-4 carried solid chevrons. (USN via San Diego Aerospace Museum)

Blue "checkerboard" tail markings on Consolidated PBY-3s of VP-41 (ex VP- 16F) over Lake Washington, Seattle, in 1938. (USN via S. Norris)

Blue tailed Vought SU-3 (9125), belonging to the squadron commander, of Marine squadron assigned to USS LEXINGTON CV-2. VS-14M served aboard SARATOGA. Both units appeared on tables of organization as US Navy units. "Pelican" insignia did not appear on earlier Vought O2U types assigned to VS-15 (Ed McCollum)

Curtiss O2C-1s of Marine Obseration Squadron Seven in Red-White-Blue markings applied to engine cowlings, wheel discs and rudders. "U.S. MARINES" spans upper wing between national insignia. VO-6M, also with O2C-1s, had similar markings. Both units omitted the "dash" between figures of the side numbers. (USMC via C. Jansson)

Fourth section of Fighting Squadron One-B, circa 1931. Absence of national insignia underwing was not uncommon. Large aircraft numbers were not usually displayed. (USN via H.S. Gann)

Unidentified crewman poses in front of Boeing O2B-1 of VO-1M aircraft at San Diego in 1927. Legend was unique to Marines. (USN via San Diego Aerospace Museum)

Fighting Squadron NINE-M (VF-9M) the third squadron of Aircraft One, Fleet Marine Force (East Coast), operated up to 24 Boeing F4B-4 aircraft and carried individual plane numbers in lieu of the three-character side number. In each three-plane section, the anti-drag ring and tail surfaces of the first aircraft were painted Red; the second White; and the third, Blue.

Earlier, Curtiss OC-2 aircraft of VO-8M and VO-10M of the West Coast Expeditionary Force (pre-Fleet Marine Force) carried distinctive markings on nose plates and wheel covers. VF-10M, the third West Coast unit, in addition to solid-color anti-drag rings and vertical fins on its Curtiss F6C-4 aircraft, was noted for applying the star of the national marking to the underside of the upper wing, and carrying a large plane number in place of the star on the lower wing. All three squadrons used the standard rudder stripes on tail surfaces.

Appearing on Marine Corps equipment only, a three-line descriptive legend was applied to each side of the fuselage, forward of the cockpit. Applied in three-inch block letters, the legend identified the squadron designation, Branch of Service and location. A typical example was:

FIGHTING SQUADRON 6 M
U.S. MARINE CORPS
NAVAL AIR STATION, SAN DIEGO

Also distinctive to the Marine Corps was the application of the Globe and Anchor emblem to all aircraft, forward of the side numbers. Two variations were utilized in the late 1920s and early 1930s, standardization was achieved in the mid-1930s when a Decalomania was issued.

For several years in the late 1920s, color was applied to the twin-float-equipped Scouting and Patrol squadrons operating Martin T3M-2 aircraft. Presumably, to identify sections, either the forward area, or afterbody of both floats were painted. Apparently, the order of colors was determined locally.

A similar application to single-float planes based aboard battleships is described in the Bureau of Aeronautics News Letter of 20 November 1926, which states: "...the forward part of the main pontoon of all number one planes of Battleship Division Three are painted Red, of BatDiv-4, White, and of BatDiv-5, Yellow. The stern of the main pontoon of all number two planes are painted the same color. It is believed that this scheme of identification will prove of great advantage both between planes in the air and between surface ships and aircraft." This reference is puzzling due to the lack of photographic evidence to confirm the application.

For the most part, Reserve units followed regular Navy practice in the application of side numbers, fuselage bands, and wing chevrons. In the late 1930s, side numbers were generally replaced with station numbers. Rudder

23

stripes were standard on tail surfaces into the 1930s, but in some instances, were replaced by solid color tail surfaces (i.e., Great Lakes: Red; New York, Blue; and Seattle, Green).

Also, in the mid-1930s, a standardized Reserve marking was adopted. This shield and anchor design, in decalcomania form was applied to the fuselage side near the cockpit area. ''Reserve Aviation'' appeared above the shield; ''U.S. Navy'' and a Navy emblem on a Blue background occupied the upper left half; a Globe and Anchor above ''U.S. MARINE CORPS,'' on a Red background the lower right half, and the name of the Reserve Base was painted on the flukes of the anchor.

Aircraft assigned to Pensacola's training squadron often carried colored tail surfaces, cowlings and large side numbers. Inasmuch as many aircraft were formally assigned to operational units, it appears likely that old squadron tail and section colors were retained until overhaul periods.

Squadron insignia are not only interesting and colorful, because of subject matter and design, but serve a most useful purpose in determining unit continuity. Unfortunately, only meager reference is made in official records to the subject, and much of it consists of reports from units describing their

LtJG Frank Akers, is the pilot of this Curtiss F6C-3 (A-7145) from Fighting Squadron Five at NAS Hampton Roads (Norfolk) in 1927. Individual insignia was unique to VF-5, scheduled for assignment to USS LEXINGTON CV-2. "Red Rippers" insignia was second for the unit. Nose application of the oversize "E" was non-standard. (USN via RAdm. F. Akers)

"Winged 2" on after fuselage applied to Curtiss JN-4H of Second Aviation Group, based at NAS North Island. Variation in "Globe and Anchor" is apparent. (USN via San Diego Aerospace Museum)

Typical Reserve markings of the mid-1930s, photographed at NAS Norfolk in 1936. Solid tail colors replaced rudder stripes at some Reserve bases and plane number was sometimes repeated on the cowling. Decalomania with unit location lettered on anchor's flukes was standard. (W.A. Riley)

24

(Above) The crash scene is NAS North Island in 1929. Boeing F2B-1 of Fighting Squadron One-B, as indicated by the "High Hat" insignia. (USN via Silver Eagles Association Collection)

Aftermath of mid-air collision between O2U-2s of Scouting Squadron Three-B. 3-S-4 was No. 8117 and 3-S-6 was No. 8105. NAS North Island on 19 April 1929. (USN via Silver Eagles Association Collection)

adopted emblems. Articles appearing in aviation and service publications were often based on informal squadron histories and interviews with squadron personnel. Specification SR-2 stated: "When an insignia has been adopted by a squadron, a copy of such insignia shall be filed with the Bureau of Aeronautics."

Many insignia reflected the squadron's class, particularly Bombing, Torpedo, and Scouting units. Patrol squadrons seemed to emphasize operating locale. No pattern can be discerned in the insignia adopted by Fighting squadrons. The most durable of all, the "High Hat" of Fighting Squadron ONE, was adopted in 1927, "just because it seemed like a good idea at the time." Presently the oldest squadron in Naval aviation, the insignia has survived numerous renumberings, and is designated VF-14 with the nickname of "Tophatters". Changes in design and/or color of insignia were made from time to time and some units adopted new emblems.

Carrier insignias were particularly appropriate. With the LANGLEY scheduled to enter service in 1922, a ships detachment was formed at Hampton Roads to train pilots in landing and take-off procedures. A design resembling the tri-color rudder stripes was adopted and placed at an angle of about 30 degrees on the fuselage side, forward of the legend "U.S.S. LANGLEY." Later, having acquired the nickname of "Covered Wagon," the insignia was modified to include a prairie schooner on the Red-White-Blue stripes.

LEXINGTON's "Minuteman" and RANGER's bust of John Paul Jones, who commanded the first RANGER in 1777, were obvious choices, and SARATOGA's "Crowing Cock" also had historical significance. Prior to World War II, ship insignias were virtually unknown, although many ships acquired nicknames. Thus, carrier insignia was applied only to aircraft of the ship's utility unit. The usual exception was SARATOGA which, for a short time, carried its insignia on a broad vertical funnel stripe. To facilitate recognition, LEXINGTON, at the same time, carried a broad horizontal stripe at the top of the funnel.

Positioning of squadron insignia on Naval aircraft was well forward of the side number, ahead of the cockpit. On flying boats, however, the insignia

Red tailed Curtiss F11C-2's of VB-1B at Long Beach in 1936. High Hat insignia identifies the squadron. (Wilford Ransom)

White tailed Curtiss BFC-2s of VB-2 (ex VF-1B High Hat aircraft) at Long Beach in 1937. High Hat insignia identifies the squadron. (Wilford Ransom)

Boeing F4B-3 of "first" VF-1 (High Hat insignia) in 1933. Unpainted cowl was typical of the unit. (Ed McCollum)

Boeing F4B-4 of "second" VF-1. Shooting Star insignia when designated VF-6 aboard ENTERPRISE in 1936. Cowl, nose plate, and band conform to painting specificatons. Controllable pitch propellers were retro-fit equipment for F4B-4s. (Ed McCollum)

often was placed aft of the wings instead of on the nose. Adoption of the Neutrality Patrol star in 1939, which was required to be placed on the nose area of aircraft involved, forced the relocation of squadron insignia on many PBY type aircraft to a position on the hull aft of the second strut.

Variations in placement were uncommon, a noteworthy exception being the application of the CPO Chevron of VF-2 (the famous enlisted pilots' squadron) on the vertical fin of the unit's FU-1s.

Inasmuch as specifications placed the Globe and Anchor emblem ahead of the side number, Marine Corps squadron insignia was usually applied on the after part of the fuselage, close to the horizontal stabilizer. Later practice was to apply the insignia on the vertical fin, and place the Branch of Service marking in its proper place below the horizontal stabilizer.

Display of squadron insignia was not mandatory, and many photographs show Navy and Marine Corps aircraft in full markings except for squadron insignia. This was particularly true of East Coast Marine Corps units.

Special purpose units, the various Alaskan Survey Expeditions being the best examples, were formed from time to time, and usually adopted an insignia which was utilized as long as the unit remained in commission.

In the early 1920s, airplanes assigned to flag officers and Commanding Officers of major aviation ships and stations, carried a standard finish and

Vought VE-7 leaves USS LANGLEY CV-1 at North Island pier. Large side letters and Red-White-Blue insignia on fuselage was typical of aircraft assigned to the Navy's first carrier. (USN via Silver Eagles Association Collection)

26

Arrow piercing USS LANGLEY marking is non-standard. Red, White and Blue stripes were adopted shortly after CV-1 entered service in 1922. Later, "Covered Wagon" was superimposed on the stripes in recognition of the nickname applied to the ship. Vought O2U-1, (A-7545) in 1926. (USN via J. W. Caler)

At the National Air Races in 1936, VO-8M carried markings in complete conformity to paint specs then in effect. Unusual, is legend applied to floatation bag cover just above the lower wing; identifying pilot, observer and plane captain. Marine Corps' "Globe and Anchor" is reduced in size. (Ed McCollum)

markings. Replicas of rank were usally painted on the fuselage or carried in brackets. Special color schemes, mostly Dark Blue fuselage painting, appeared in the mid-twenties. Occasionally, a personal flag of an Admiral (White stars on a Blue field) was flown from the interplane struts.

In May of 1934, the Chief of the Bureau of Aeronautics issued specific instructions regulating the "Painting of Special Aircraft." Two color schemes were described: (1) for flag officers; and (2) for Commanding Officers of aircraft carriers, tenders, Fleet Air Bases and major Air Stations. The letter included detailed instructions relative to the application of Blue enamel to metal parts and fabric surfaces, the use of Aluminum paint, and the fittings to be chromium plated. A "Tentative Process Specification for Painting

Replacement aircraft for VMF-2 lacks cowl painting and plane number. Red Lion insignia was later modified to show unit's performance in the defense of Wake Island in late 1941 when they were designated VMF-211. Plane is Grumman F3F-2. Note Marine Corps insignia on fuselage just below the windscreen. 1938. (W.L. Swisher)

Loening OL-8As of the 1929 Alaskan Survey on the ramp at San Diego. Number one was JUNEAU and number three was PETERSBURG. Special insignia is repeated on helmets of pilots and crew. National insignia does not appear underwing. (USN via Silver Eagles Association Collection)

Beautifully detailed "command" aircraft of RAdm W.A. Moffett, Chief, Bureau of Aeronautics. Photographed at NAS Anacostia in April of 1926, the Navy Department seal, two-star plaque and unusual 'eagle' on highly polished fuel tank are clearly visible. Vought UO-1, No. A-6896. (USN via H.S. Gann)

Two-line legend forward of cockpit identifies this Boeing O2B-1, No. A-6908, as: "Maj. E.H. Brainerd, O-in-C, USMC Aviation." Major's oak leaf insignia appears just aft of the radiator. (USN via San Diego Aerospace Museum).

Boeing F4B-1 (A-8133) in overall Blue paint scheme assigned to Asst. Secy. of the Navy, for Air, Douglas S. Ingalls in 1930. Fin appears to be White with Blue stripes with the serial numbers in a vertical alignment. Four Blue stars and anchor on White Field is unusual. (USN via H.S. Gann)

Beautifully detailed "command" aircraft painted in accordance with BuAero letter Aer-D-158-RC of 5 May 1934. Fuselage, wing struts, strut cuffs and wheel fairings are "Admiral Blue" with tail surfaces in aluminum. Fuselage tank straps and miscelleneous trim and hardware are finished in chromium. Letters on fabric finish are Black on Aluminum and Aluminum on Blue. The wheel fairing "is decorated by painting the figure on the Blue enamel with Gold leaf and sprinkIng with aluminum powder before it dries." The directive further stated: "To avoid the feather edge at the juncture of aluminum figures and letters and the Blue, a narrow Red stripe should be traced at the junction line." (USN via H. S. Gann)

The six Vought O2U-2s transferred to the Coast Guard from the Navy in 1934 and 1935 did not carry the standard paint scheme. Navy Bureau Number (8109) appeared below the model designation on the rudder. In the 1936 re-numbering program, No. 303 became V119. (USCG via T.E. Doll)

No. 9347, believed to be the first of three Douglas RD-2s delivered in 1933. This aircraft was especially configured for possible use by President Franklin D. Roosevelt. Actual assignment as a "presidential aircraft" cannot be determined. (USN via T.E. Doll)

Boeing F3B-1, No. 7738 (in vertical alignment), carrying Captain's shoulder board on the fuselage, is painted in conformity with directive for painting of special aircraft, except for wheel fairing design. (Wilford Ransom).

NAF built Curtiss TR-1 (ex-TS-1), No. A-6303, with temporarily assigned "race number" was flown to first place in the 1922 Curtiss Marine Trophy Race by Lt. A.W. "Jake" Gorton at Detroit on 8 October. "TR-1" is lettered on outboard struts. (USN via H.S. Gann)

White fuselage band and reversed wing chevron are outlined in Black on this Douglas PD-1 of VP-6, as is White "E" with "MB" for excellence in machine guns and bombing. "Large as possible" side numbers are typical of application to patrol aircraft in the mid-1930s. Solid Blue tail color replaced rudder stripes in 1934. (USN via H.S. Gann)

Special Aircraft." issued in August of 1934 by the Naval Aircraft Factory, referred to the Blue enamel as "Admiral Blue."

For flag officers, the entire fuselage, as well as anti-drag ring or engine cowling, and wheel fairings, was painted Dark Blue. Wings and tail surfaces retained the standard finish; the tail group usually being Aluminum, but occasionally carrying rudder stripes. An exception was the Curtiss SOC-3 of C-in-C, U.S. FLEET, with Blue tail surfaces.

For Commanding Officers, the N.A.F. directive stated: "Airplanes requiring Class II color scheme shall have the forward section of the fuselage covering painted Admiral Blue to just aft of the trailing edge of the wing root fillet at the lower longeron and the Blue area shall be "faired in" as shown on Figure II."

For both painting schemes: "Letters and/or figures on fabric shall be Black on Aluminum or Aluminum on Admiral Blue. To avoid the feather edge at the junction of Aluminum letters and figures and the Blue, a narrow Red stripe shall be traced at the junction line." Also, "A streamline shape shall be applied to the outside surface of each wheel faring...on the Admiral Blue enamel with Gold leaf size...sprinkled with Aluminum powder before drying."

For Air Group Commanders, a diagonal stripe, in the same color as that assigned to the air group, was applied to the fuselage, from just behind the engine to the lower wing fillet. The legend "Air Group Commander" over the carriers name was placed below the cockpit. In the late 1930s, several experimental patrol type aircraft were utilized as "flying flagships" with the title of the command lettered on the hull in Black paint.

Aircraft entered in the Schneider Cup and Pulitzer Trophy contests were often painted in special schemes and usually carried temporarily applied race numbers. Aircraft participating in the National Air Races were usually operational types, again with temporary race numbers painted on fuselage side and/or vertical tail surfaces.

Several special markings, usually related to ordanance and communication competitions, were applied to aircraft. One of the oldest was the Gunnery

Trophy Pennant, awarded to one squadron of each class for excellence in gunnery competition, usually applied forward of the unit markings in Red paint. Relatively uncommon, the Communications "C" was also placed forward of the unit markings, in White paint.

Pilots who qualified in the annual Individual Battle Practice (IBP) exercise could place a Gunnery "E" on their aircraft. The marking was placed foward of the unit marking near the cockpit, in White paint, sometimes outlined in Black. Slanting stripes, known as "hashmarks" were placed below the "E" for subsequent requalifications. More than three were very rare. A small "B" for Bombing, or an "M" for Machine Gun (both infrequently) sometimes appeared either below or just behind the "E", usually in White.

The seldom-seen "Shellback" Turtle was applied to aircraft which had flown across the Equator. The device was usually painted on the upper part of the vertical fin, but did appear forward of the cockpit. A slanting White stripe was usually applied to the left side of the vertical fin on low-wing monoplane types to assist the Landing Signal Officer. It was common practice to place the name of the pilot, and often that of the plane captain, in small block letters just below the cockpit.

Ambulance modifications of DH-4 type aircraft carried special "Red Cross" markings on the fuselage side, with one having large crosses on the top wing in place of the national insignia. However, two Loening XHL-1's purchased in the early 1930s were not specially marked as ambulance aircraft.

In the early 1920s, American flags and commission pennants were flown by H-16 and F-5-L flying boats. At anchor, the Union Jack was flown from a staff at the bow. The procedure was limited in application and appears to have been a perogative of command.

Each Curtiss F9C-2 "Sparrowhawk" fighting aircraft attached to U.S.S. MACON in 1933 was marked as a section leader, with rudder stripes on the tail surfaces. In 1934, solid Black was assigned as a tail color, section leader markings being retained.

From time to time, various tests of low-visibility and camouflage paint schemes were conducted by fleet activities. As a rule, water-soluble paint in various shades of Gray and Blue were applied in an over-all or combination scheme to operational aircraft.

In November of 1935, one section of airplanes in each of 11 squadrons (VB, VF, VS, VT, and VP) were camouflaged and observed by various fleet units. Subsequent tests were conducted with Curtiss BFC-2 airplanes at San Diego. These, and other tests, formed the basis for the various camouflage paint schemes used in World War II.

The "Broad Command" pennant on the nose of NAF PN-7, No. A-6616, assigned to Scouting Squadon One in 1925 is unique. Insignia has not been identified. (USN via H.S. Gann)

Two F-5Ls of the East Coast Scouting Squadron, at anchor in a Carribean port, display the Union Jack on the bow. (E.T. Garvey)

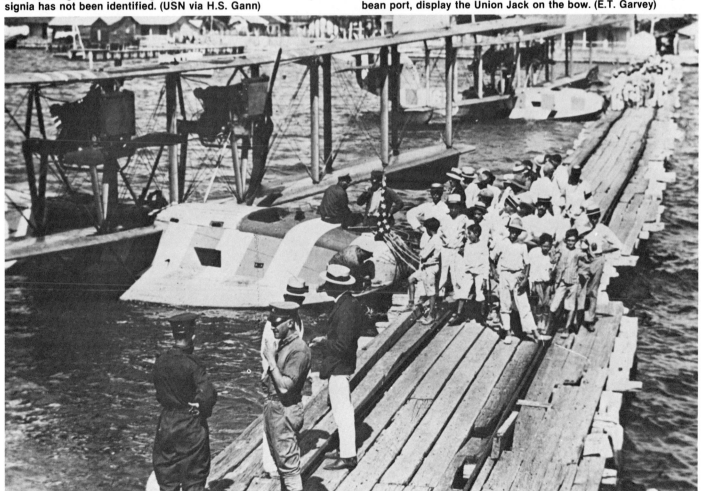

Shakedown cruise on USS RANGER, CV-4, was to South American ports. Winged turtle marking was applied to aircraft that had flown over the equator on the 1934 cruise. Application appeared on vertical fins and various positions on the fuselage. Photo taken in 1936. (Ed McCollum)

Curtiss F9C-2 "hooked-on" fighters assigned to rigid airships AKRON and MACON carried a variety of markings. Here, No. 9059 has full section markings (Black) with fuselage band and reversed wing chevron outlined in White. Five other aircraft of the MACON's HTA unit were similarly marked. Fins on front of wheel covers were to prevent carrier deck wires from overriding the landing gear. Carrier operations of F9C-2s were experimental. Rudder stripes were later replaced by Black as a unit tail color. (USN via H.S. Gann)

Douglas TBD-1, No. 0353, at NAS Pensacola in 1938. Both current and obsolescent types carried large side numbers. Information on paint-ing of cowlings, fuselage bands and tail surfaces suggests a system of markings based on unit organization but is not confirmed by documents. (USN via D. Bruce Van Alstine)

Fleet Squadron Re-Organization
1 July 1937

INSIGNIA	OLD NUMBER	SHIP	TAIL COLOR	NEW NUMBER	SHIP	TAIL COLOR
Bellerophon or Pegasus	VB-5B	LEXINGTON	Green	VB-2	LEXINGTON	Yellow
CPO Chevron	VF-2B	LEXINGTON	Yellow	VF-2	LEXINGTON	Yellow
Indian Head in Circle	VS-3B	LEXINGTON	Yellow	VS-2	LEXINGTON	Yellow
Bombman on Torpedo	VB-1B	RANGER	Yellow	VT-2	LEXINGTON	Yellow
High Hat	VB-2B	SARATOGA	Red	VB-3	SARATOGA	White
Felix the Cat	VF-6B	SARATOGA	White	VF-3	SARATOGA	White
Pointer Dog	VS-2B	SARATOGA	White	VS-3	SARATOGA	White
Dragon on Torpedo	VT-2B	SARATOGA	Red	VT-3	SARATOGA	White
Black Panther	VB-3B	LEXINGTON	Green	VB-4	RANGER	Green
The Red Rippers	VF-5B	RANGER	Blue	VF-4	RANGER	Green
Duck on Pontoons	VS-1B	RANGER	Green	VS-41	RANGER	Green
The Dodo Bird	VS-4B	SARATOGA	White	VS-42	RANGER	Green
Winged Satan's Head	VB-7B	YORKTOWN	Red	VB-5	YORKTOWN	Red
Eagle on Star (1)	VF-7B	YORKTOWN	Red	VF-5	YORKTOWN	Red
Man-o-War Bird	VS-7B	YORKTOWN	Red	VS-5	YORKTOWN	Red
Valkyrie	VT-7B	YORKTOWN	Red	VT-5	YORKTOWN	Red
Mountain Goat	VB-8B	ENTERPRISE	Blue	VB-6	ENTERPRISE	Blue
Shooting Star	VF-8B	ENTERPRISE	Blue	VF-6	ENTERPRISE	Blue
Aztec Headdress	VS-8B	ENTERPRISE	Blue	VS-6	ENTERPRISE	Blue
Great White Albatross	VT-8B	ENTERPRISE	Blue	VT-6	ENTERPRISE	Blue
Bat on S in Circle (2)	VS-5B	---------	Blue	VCS-2	---------	Blue
Winged Seahorse	VS-6B	---------	Red	VCS-3	---------	Red
(Unknown)	VS-9S	---------	White	VCS-4	---------	White
Duck on Catapult	VS-10S	---------	Yellow	VCS-5	---------	Yellow
Flying Fish	VS-11S	---------	Black	VCS-6	---------	Black
Wing and Binoculars	VS-12S	---------	Green	VCS-7	---------	Black
Four Dolphins	VS-14S	---------	Black	VCS-8	---------	Black

(1) Was VF-3 on RANGER with Green tail. For a few months, during the formation of the ENTERPRISE Air Group it became VF-7B.
(2) Cruiser Scouting Squadrons added a "C" for Cruiser to their squadron designation. The four VO, Battleship Observation, squadrons remained the same, dropped the B suffix letter.

Above date courtesy "US Navy Aircraft 1921 - 1941", Aviation Historical Publications, William T. Larkins 1961.

National Insignia Chronology

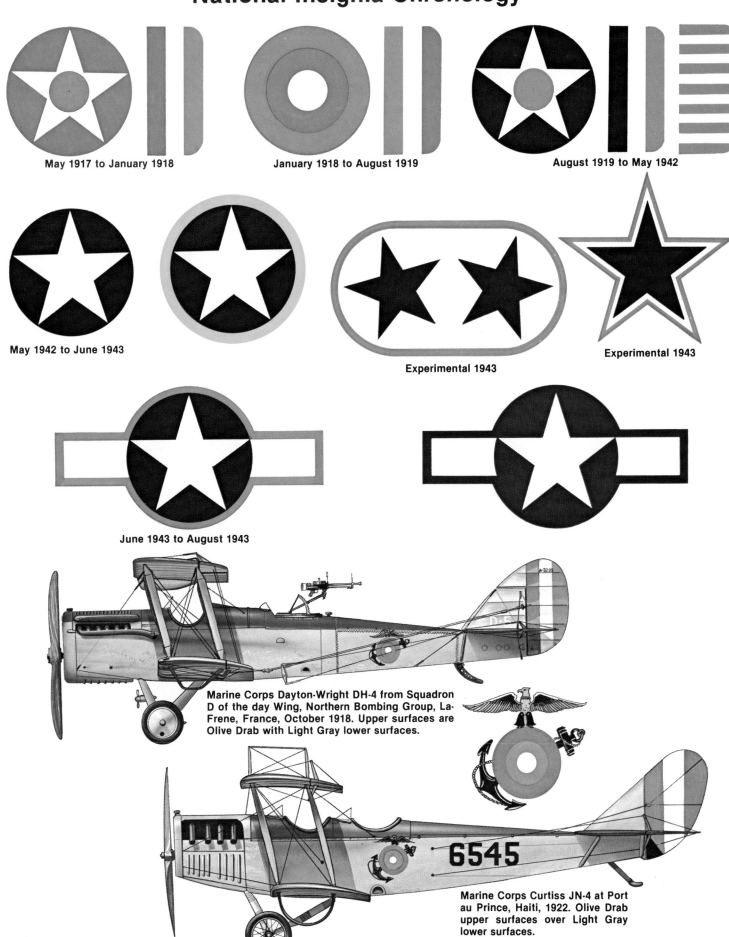

May 1917 to January 1918

January 1918 to August 1919

August 1919 to May 1942

May 1942 to June 1943

Experimental 1943

Experimental 1943

June 1943 to August 1943

Marine Corps Dayton-Wright DH-4 from Squadron D of the day Wing, Northern Bombing Group, La-Frene, France, October 1918. Upper surfaces are Olive Drab with Light Gray lower surfaces.

Marine Corps Curtiss JN-4 at Port au Prince, Haiti, 1922. Olive Drab upper surfaces over Light Gray lower surfaces.

LIGHTER-THAN-AIR

Generally speaking, all lighter-than-air equipment, kite, balloons, spherical free balloons, non-rigid airships, and rigid airships, received either a Silver or Aluminum finish.

Painting specifications of the 1920s and early 1930s described in detail the placement, size, and color of the national insignia, tail surface painting, branch of service marking, and other prescribed identification letters and numbers. Later, specifications were in general terms, and required the contractor to "submit for approval on all production contracts, a drawing or drawings showing the size and location of each type of marking required."

Two national insignia (stars) were placed on spherical balloons. Their size was five feet in diameter. The words "U.S. NAVY" in letters 54 inches high, were painted on the envelope. Class designation letters and figures and building letters and numbers were applied in three-inch letters in Insignia Blue paint. Variations in placement were common. Kite balloons were painted in similar style.

On non-rigid airships, five-foot stars were applied on the envelope, one on top and one on the bottom, toward the nose. "U.S. NAVY" and model designation appeared on each side of the envelope in 54 inch letters. Other required markings were applied in three-inch letters in Insignia Blue paint. Rudder stripes were standard on tail surfaces.

Four rigid airships were operated by the Navy between 1923 and 1935. Painting specifications simply stated that insignia and markings "shall be prescribed in each case by the Bureau of Aeronautics and will be shown on the BuAero detailed drawings for each airship." With some variations, each carried the star on each side forward of the tail surfaces; "U.S. NAVY" on each side, amidships; and the name near the horizontal stabilizer.

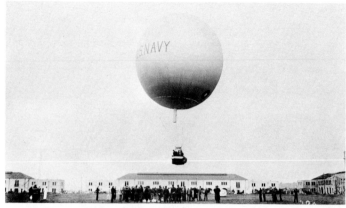

Free balloon at NAS San Diego in early 1920. Enlisted men's barracks is in the background. World War One cockade is noteworthy. (USN via San Diego Aerospace Museum)

Goodyear F-1, No. A-6348, lacks rudder stripes. However, "U.S. NAVY" and airship designation is typical application to non-rigid airships of all periods. Examination of photographs indicates that national insignia was frequently not applied on nose. (USN via San Diego Aerospace Museum)

USS SHENANDOAH ZR-1 off coast of California in 1924. National insignia on side is not in proper alignment. At one time "ZR-1" was painted on the nose. Rudder stripes and national insignia were applied on LOS ANGELES, AKRON and MAKON in similiar method as SHENANDOAH. (USN via John W. Caler)

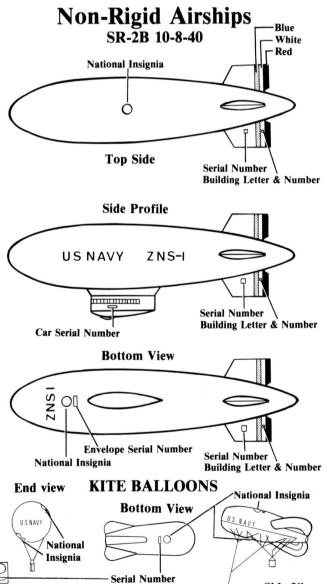

Non-Rigid Airships
SR-2B 10-8-40

National Insignia

Blue
White
Red

Top Side

Serial Number
Building Letter & Number

Side Profile

US NAVY   ZNS-1

Car Serial Number

Serial Number
Building Letter & Number

Bottom View

ZNS-1

Envelope Serial Number

National Insignia

Serial Number
Building Letter & Number

End view

US NAVY

National Insignia

KITE BALLOONS

Bottom View

National Insignia

US NAVY

Serial Number

Side View

Free Balloons

WORLD WAR TWO

SR-2B

On 19 March 1940, the Bureau of Aeronautics issued a set of detailed instructions regarding the proper placement and size of the United States national aviation insignia to be applied to the fuselages and hulls of US Navy aircraft participating in the Neutrality Patrol.

This directive, AER-E-255-HY, QW-19, F-39-1, Technical Note 6-40, was intended to be a supplement to the first order covering the application of the Neutrality Patrol star that was issued in December of 1939. The basic color scheme of United States Naval aircraft remained as before except for the addition of the Neutrality Patrol Star insignia.

The directive of 19 March called out the following:

(a) BG-1 Airplanes — Center a two-foot diameter star insignia on the engine accessory cowling as far forward as possible.

(b) SOC-1, SOC-2, SOC-3, SON-1 Airplanes — Center a two-foot diameter star insignia on the accessory cowling with the upper circumference about 5 inches below the top of the cowling.

(c) SBU-1 and SBU-2 Airplanes — Locate a two-foot diameter star insignia on the engine cowling so that the after edge is tangent to the after edge of the side cowl, and the center is equidistant from the upper and lower edge of each side panel of the cowl.

(d) SB2U-1 and SB2U-2 Airplanes — locate a two-foot diameter star insignia on the engine cowling, so that it's center is 2 feet aft of the forward edge of the cowl panel, part number CV-42859, and 14 inches below the upper edge of the side panel of the cowl.

(e) F2F-1, F3F-1, F3F-2, F3F-3 Airplanes — Locate a two-foot diameter star insignia on the fuselage between the two cabane wires between stations 2 and 4. The center of the insignia is to be 11 3/4 inches aft of station 2, and 12 1/4 inches below a line joining the lower ends of the cabane struts.

(f) J2F-1, J2F-2, J2F-3, J2F-4 Airplanes — Center a three-foot diameter star in line with the vertical cabane strut, with the lower edge of the star approximately 23 inches above the step, adjacent to the upper edge of the wheel well.

(g) PBY-1, PBY-2, PBY-3, PBY-4 Airplanes — Locate a three-foot diameter star insignia so that it's lower circumference is approximately 4 inches above the mooring platform, between the turret and windshield, with the after circumference tangent to the outer edge of the reinforcement at the pilot's ventilator.

(h) P2Y-2 and P2Y-3 Airplanes — Locate a three-foot diameter star insignia so that it's lower circumference is three inches above the chine edge and it's after edge is approximately one inch forward of the forward edge of the bow step.

Note: Where the insignia is to be located on the engine or accessory cowling, it is satisfactory for the star to project into squadron nose markings, provided a contrasting border is also applied at the intersection.

On 8 October 1940, the Bureau issued SR-2B another in the SR-2 series of painting directives. The instructions set forth in SR-2B codified many of the practices already in use before the issuance of the 8 October document. Carrier tail colors were listed as follows:

USS Saratoga, CV-3	White
USS Lexington, CV-2	Lemon Yellow
USS Ranger, CV-4	Willow Green
USS Yorktown, CV-5	Insignia Red
USS Enterprise, CV-6	True Blue
USS Wasp, CV-7	Black

The section colors which identified the position of any given airplane within the squadron were applied on the nose of the cowling, forward of the engine on an aircraft powered by an air cooled engine, or in the case of an airplane powered by a liquid cooled engine, a band 12 inches wide was applied beginning at the nose of the airplane.

On the wings, a chevron was to be applied according to the section color for the aircraft. Where possible, the chevron was to be applied so that the apex of the chevron aligned with the center of the pilot's cockpit. In the case of monoplanes, where the chevron marking on the wing terminated at the leading edge of the wing, the chevron was to be extended, to a point on the undersurface of the wing to approximately 5% of the chord from the leading edge.

Application of the section color to the airplane's fuselage occurred only in the case of the section leader. A colored band approximately 20 inches wide was applied around the fuselage in a position forward of the service markings, i.e. US NAVY or US MARINES. Section colors were detailed as follows:

1st section...a/c #1-2-3	Insignia Red
2nd section...a/c #4-5-6	White
3rd section...a/c #7-8-9	True Blue
4th section...a/c #10-11-12	Black
5th section...a/c #13-14-15	Willow Green
6th section...a/c #16-17-18	Lemon Yellow

The United States Navy was well represented at the 1939-40 New York World's Fair. Here, in the Aviation Building on the Avenue of Transportation, is a Curtiss SBC-4 (1269) from the Reserve base in New York, painted as a VS-2 squadron commander's aircraft, 2-S-1. A Vought SB2U-2 is seen in the colors of the USS WASP's VS-72 number four aircraft, 72-S-4. "Wings of Defense" was the theme of the presentation. (USN/National Archives)

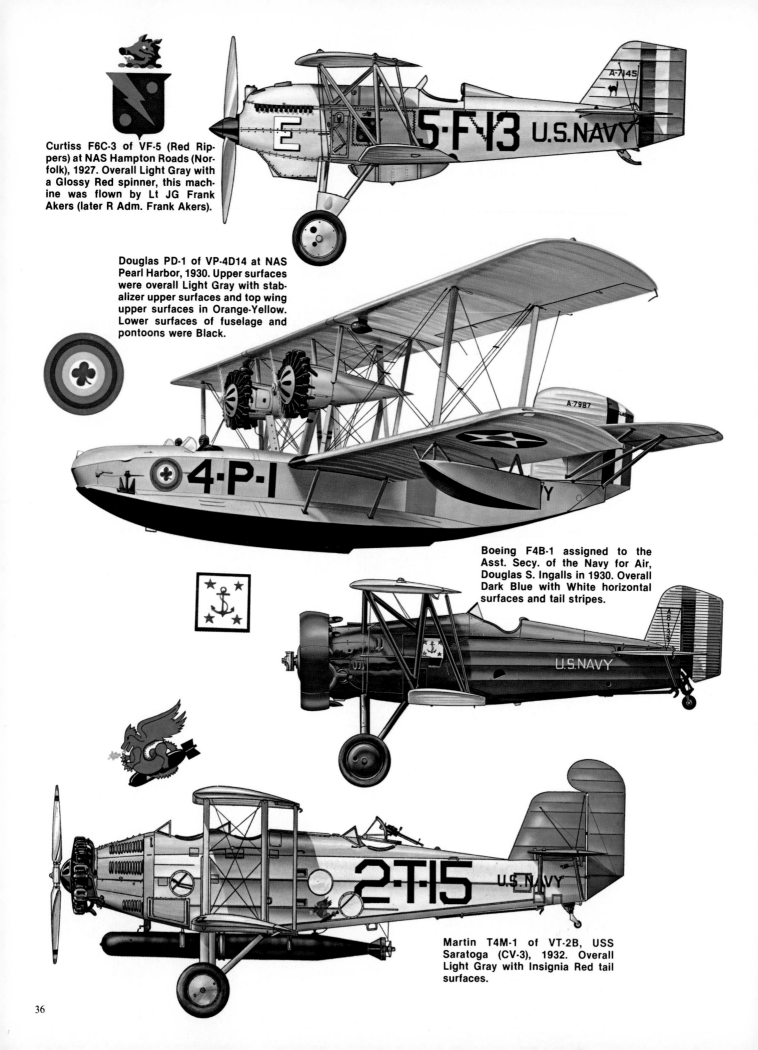

Curtiss F6C-3 of VF-5 (Red Rippers) at NAS Hampton Roads (Norfolk), 1927. Overall Light Gray with a Glossy Red spinner, this machine was flown by Lt JG Frank Akers (later R Adm. Frank Akers).

Douglas PD-1 of VP-4D14 at NAS Pearl Harbor, 1930. Upper surfaces were overall Light Gray with stabalizer upper surfaces and top wing upper surfaces in Orange-Yellow. Lower surfaces of fuselage and pontoons were Black.

Boeing F4B-1 assigned to the Asst. Secy. of the Navy for Air, Douglas S. Ingalls in 1930. Overall Dark Blue with White horizontal surfaces and tail stripes.

Martin T4M-1 of VT-2B, USS Saratoga (CV-3), 1932. Overall Light Gray with Insignia Red tail surfaces.

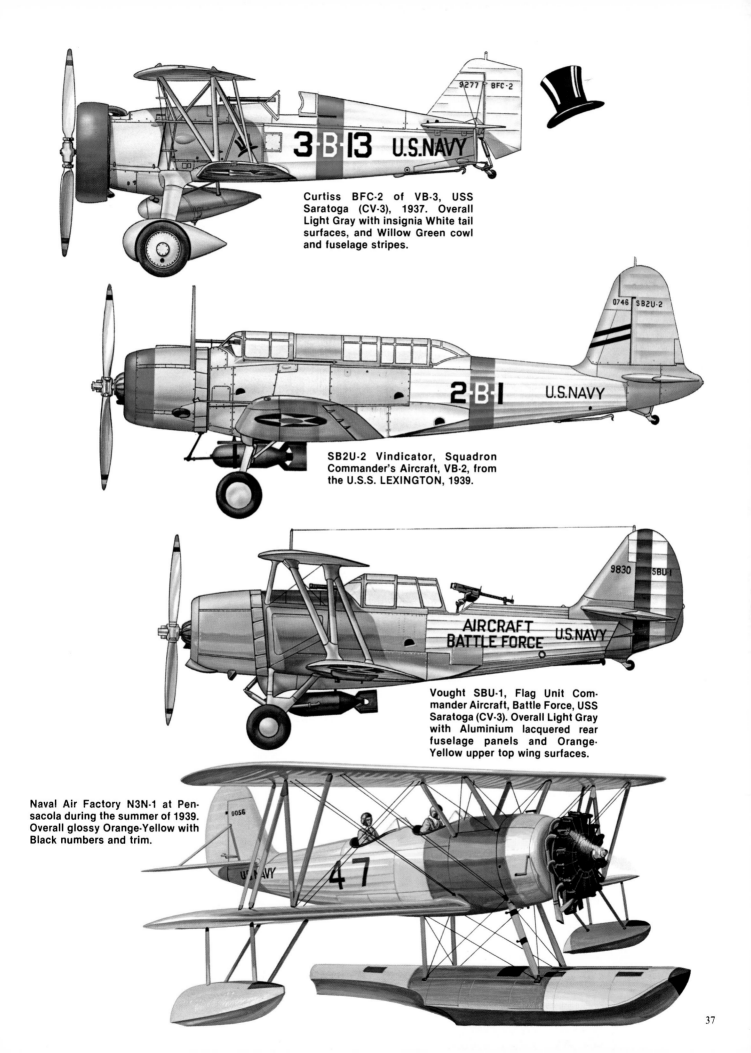

Curtiss BFC-2 of VB-3, USS Saratoga (CV-3), 1937. Overall Light Gray with insignia White tail surfaces, and Willow Green cowl and fuselage stripes.

SB2U-2 Vindicator, Squadron Commander's Aircraft, VB-2, from the U.S.S. LEXINGTON, 1939.

Vought SBU-1, Flag Unit Commander Aircraft, Battle Force, USS Saratoga (CV-3). Overall Light Gray with Aluminium lacquered rear fuselage panels and Orange-Yellow upper top wing surfaces.

Naval Air Factory N3N-1 at Pensacola during the summer of 1939. Overall glossy Orange-Yellow with Black numbers and trim.

Grumman J2F-3 (1587) amphibian illustrates well the Neutrality Patrol star adopted by carrier aircraft operating in the Atlantic in March of 1940. Also shown is the Blue, White and Red vertical rudder stripes applied to utility planes during that time period. (USN/National Archives)

(Below) This F3F-1 sports a variety of markings. The rudder designation "F3" is incomplete, the number "34" on the fuselage was applied after it arrived at Miami, where it became a trainer on 10 February 1941, and it still retains the Neutrality Patrol star. Tail color appears to be Black, the last operational carrier squadron it served with was VF-7. Prior to VF-7 this F3F-1 served with VF-6B (SARATOGA) and VF-4 (RANGER). It went on to serve as a trainer at NAS Miami and with the Reserve at NRAB Floyd Bennett Field, New York. On 6 November 1942 this airplane was shipped to the Aviation Maintenance School in Memphis, Tennessee where it remained throughout WW II as a training aid. (Capt. L.E. Dailey, USMC)

Grumman F2F-1 (9641) showing the Black tail color assigned to aircraft of the USS WASP CV-7 in 1940. Fuselage coding, as outlined in SR-2b, is seen to advantage on these aircraft. Lower half of cowling is painted Black with White outline. (Capt. L.E. Dailey, USMC)

(Below) By June of 1940 VF-7 had replaced their F2F-1s with F3F-1s. Seen here is 7-F-12, (0242) with VF-7. "Blue Burglar Wasp" squadron insignia located on the fuselage just aft of the Neutrality Patrol star. Black wing chevron is visible on topside of upper wing. Lower half of cowling is painted Black with White outline. (R. Seybil)

(Above) Scouting Squadron 72's Vought SB2U-2s illustrate the application of the Neutrality Patrol star to this type aircraft. Shown here to advantage is the prop tips painted with three 4" bands of Insignia Red, Orange-Yellow and Insignia Blue. The top half of the cowling is painted Willow Green, identifying this plane as 72-S-14. (Capt. L.E. Dailey, USMC)

(Above Right) Good view of VS-72s "Centaur Vampire" insignia and Individual Battle Practice "E". (Capt. L.E. Dailey, USMC)

(Right) January 1941 photo of VF-72's Grumman F4F-3s. The F4F only appeared in the colorful high-visibility paint scheme for a short time; December 1940 to March 1941. Both VF-41 and VF-42 (RANGER), and VF-72 (WASP) carried the Neutrality Patrol stars on their F4Fs but applied them in different locations. VF-72 painted the star in the position shown in the photograph, while the RANGER F4Fs applied the star on the fuselage just above the leading edge of the wing. (Capt. Brown via D. Bruce Van Alstine)

VF-41 "Red Rippers" F4F-3 (1850) at the Grumman factory before the application of the number "1" to complete the fuselage code. The "Red Ripper" insignia has been applied to the fuselage just below the cockpit, somewhat larger than the recommended six inch maximum, which would soon become the standard with the adoption of the overall Light Grey low-visibility paint scheme. The model designation and Bureau number applied to the aircraft's rudder and fin were to be three inches in height. Neutrality Patrol star on this F4F-3 is in a different position than star on VF-72 F4F-3s. This is probably due to the fact that the 19 March 1940 directive did not list star location details for the F4F-3 airplane. Most other types were covered in directive. Tail color for RANGER planes was Willow Green at this time. (Capt. W.E. Scarborough, USN, Ret.)

The section leader's aircraft, carrying fuselage bands, were aircraft numbered 1,4,7,10,13 and 16.

The service marking, US NAVY - US MARINES, was to be painted on each side of the fuselage midway between the top and bottom and parallel to the longitudinal axis of the airplane, with the last letter located approximately 12 inches from the rudder hinge. The letter size of the service marking was to be of an appropriate size so as to provide a neat appearance consistant with the space available and congruous with the other markings. The minimum size of the letters was 4 inches.

Fuselage coding, 3-T-16, etc., was applied to the side of the fuselage of each airplane. For example, the fuselage coding on the Douglas TBD-1 was 20 inches high while the fuselage coding on the Grumman F4F-3 was 12 inches. The breakdown of the fuselage coding was as follows:

Example...3-T-16

The number 3 designated the squadron number. In this case the squadron was Torpedo Squadron 3 attached to the aircraft car-

rier USS SARATOGA CV-3.

The letter T was called the mission letter. In this case it designated "Torpedo". Others used, depending on the mission, were F for fighters; B for bombing; S for scouting; J for utility; O for observation; N for training; P for patrol; R for transport squadrons (multi-engined); G for transport squadrons (single engined) and M for miscellaneous.

The last number in the coding represented the individual aircraft number.

Fuselage coding was applied with Glossy Black lacquer. The color of the mission letter on the section leader's aircraft depended on the color of the fuselage band; White on Red and Blue; Black on White, Green and Yellow. Fuselage coding was applied forward of the service marking and was to be in such a position that the centers of the two groups were on a horizontal axial plane. All fuselage code characters were to be of the modified vertical block style, uniform in shape and size.

United States Marine Corps
Non-Standard Tail Markings 1929-1935

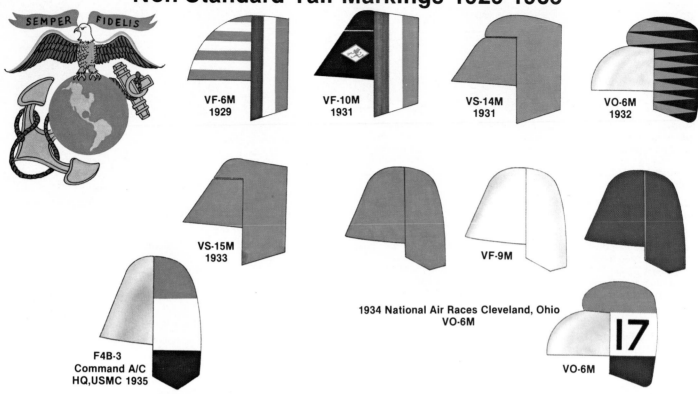

VF-6M
1929

VF-10M
1931

VS-14M
1931

VO-6M
1932

VS-15M
1933

VF-9M

1934 National Air Races Cleveland, Ohio
VO-6M

F4B-3
Command A/C
HQ,USMC 1935

VO-6M

Standard Tail Markings
USN-USMC-USCG 1935-1941

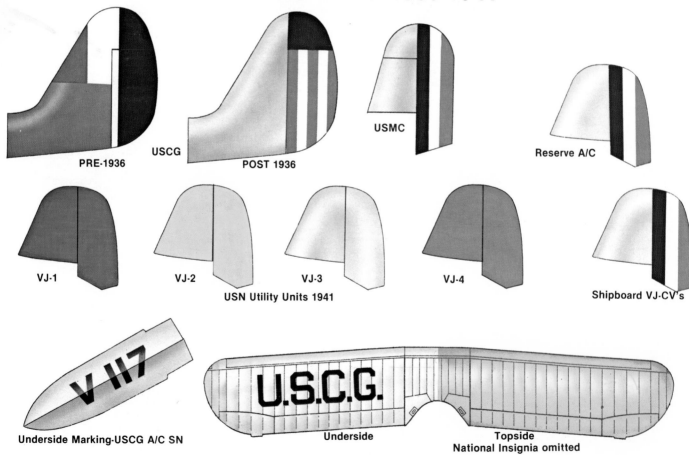

PRE-1936

USCG

POST 1936

USMC

Reserve A/C

VJ-1

VJ-2

VJ-3

VJ-4

USN Utility Units 1941

Shipboard VJ-CV's

V 117

Underside Marking-USCG A/C SN

U.S.C.G.

Underside

Topside
National Insignia omitted

Typical Both Sides, R-LH

USN BB-CA-CL Aviation Unit Tail Markings
Per SR-2B of 8 October 1940

VO-1

VO-2

VO-3

VO-4

VO-5

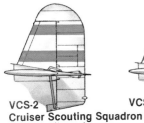
VCS-2
Cruiser Scouting Squadron

VCS-3

VCS-4

VCS-5

VCS-6

VCS-7

VCS-8

VCS-9

USS Raleigh CL-7

USS Detroit CL-8

USS Richmond CL-9

BB-CA-CL Cowling Markings SOC A/C

2 plane sections
CL's

AC 1

AC 2

AC - 3-4 white
AC - 5-6 true blue
AC - 7-8 black
AC - 9-10 willow green

Light Cruisers, CL-4 to CL-13
Omaha Class only

4 plane sections
CA's & CL's

AC 1

AC 2

AC 3

AC 4

AC - 5-6 7-8 white
AC - 9-10-11-12 true blue
AC - 13-14-15-16 black
AC - 17-18-19-20 willow green

CA = Heavy Cruiser

3 plane sections
Battleships (BB)

AC 1

AC 2

AC 3

AC - 4-5-6 white
AC - 7-8-9 true blue
AC - 10-11-12 black
AC - 13-14-15 willow green

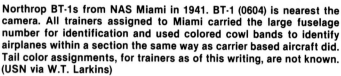

Northrop BT-1s from NAS Miami in 1941. BT-1 (0604) is nearest the camera. All trainers assigned to Miami carried the large fuselage number for identification and used colored cowl bands to identify airplanes within a section the same way as carrier based aircraft did. Tail color assignments, for trainers as of this writing, are not known. (USN via W.T. Larkins)

(Above Right) Training TBD-1 at NAS Pensacola after mis-hap on 6 November 1940. This TBD-1 (0354) went on to serve with VT-3 and was lost during that unit's participation in the Battle of Midway, 4 June 1942. Overall Aluminum varnish and individual aircraft number on fuselage are the only features of this Pensacola trainer. (USN/National Archives via D. Bruce Van Alstine)

(Right) Command OS2U-1 (1691). Delivered to the Commander-in-Chief, US Fleet aboard the USS PENNSYLVANIA BB-38, on 4 October 1940. This OS2U featured "Admiral Blue" fuselage wih Aluminum varnish finish on wings, floats and tail surfaces. "U.S. FLEET" and "U.S. NAVY" in White lettering. Topside of wings were Orange-Yellow. (USN)

(Right) Example of Air Group Commander's stripe as applied to bi-plane fuselage. The plane, Curtiss SBC-3 (0527), was YORKTOWN's Air Group Commander's aircraft. Tail color and fuselage stripe are Insignia Red. (W.T. Larkins)

(Right) Example of CAG stripe as applied to low wing monoplanes. Commander Ranger Air Group SB2U-1 features Willow Green tail color and fuselage stripe. Because this aircraft served as the Air Group Commander's, it carried no wing chevron or section color. Face of propeller was painted flat Black to prevent glare. Diagonal stripes on vertical fin were used as an aid in landing the plane during carrier operations by the ship's Landing Signal Officer. These stripes were Insignia Red in color. (James C. Fahey)

42

(Above) Bent and battered Douglas TBD-1 illustrates extremely large "E" with accompanying letters "BT" for proficiency in bombing and torpedo bombing. This TBD was involved in a mishap on 26 January 1940 and was flown by C.E. Ziegler, AMM2/c (NAP). Fuselage coding was 3-T-8, BuNo. 0291. (USN/National Archives via D. Bruce Van Alstine)

(Above Right) Example of wing chevron as applied to TBD-1 of VT-6 in 1940. In this case the chevron was Insignia Red with a one inch border applied to each side. Bottom half of engine cowling also painted Insignia Red with one inch Insignia White outline. Small type "E" and smaller "T" is shown as well as VT-6's insignia. Fuselage coding was 6-T-3, BuNo. 1505. This TBD was lost on 4 June 1942 during the Battle of Midway. (USN/National Archives via D. Bruce Van Alstine)

(Right) The "Classic" model of the SNJ series, the -2. The Marine Corps insignia adorns fuselage with rudder displaying vertical Insignia Blue, White and Red stripes directed by SR-2b for USMC aircraft. Fuselage is painted Aluminum with top surface of wings painted glossy Orange-Yellow. All exterior lettering is Black except the White "S" on the Blue rudder stripe. At the time, 1940, this SNJ-2 (2032) was assigned to the Base Air Detachment at the Marine Corps base at Quantico, Virginia. (Capt. L.E. Dailey, USMC)

(Right) Very rare photograph of Douglas SBD-2 painted in pre-WW II USN color scheme. First SBDs (-1s) were delivered to the Marine Corps in the colorful scheme but the first SBDs for the Navy were believed to have only been delivered in the overall Non-specular Light Grey scheme. In this Douglas factory photo we see that at least one SBD-2 was painted in the USN pre-war scheme. Aircraft is marked 2-B-4 with Insignia White fuselage band and Lemon Yellow Tail surfaces (for USS LEXINGTON CV-2) and Orange-Yellow top wing surfaces. BuNo. 2108. (Douglas Aircraft via H.S. Gann)

(Below Right) This Lockheed XR40-1 (1441) was the only example of the civil Model 14 airliner used by the Navy. It was assigned to NAS Anacostia, D.C. as a high-speed staff transport. As can be observed, the model designation and Bureau Number were applied to both sides of the vertical fin and rudder. Four star Admiral's placard was Dark Blue with Gold stars. (Capt. L.E. Dailey, USMC)

(Below) Lockheed JO-2 (1049) shows vertical tail stripes applied to both inside and outside surfaces of rudder. Two-star general's placard, just behind the cowl indicated the aircraft was in use by a Marine Corps general officer. Propeller spinner and de-icer boots on leading edges of wings and horizontal stabilizer were Black rubberized material. (Capt. L.E. Dailey, USMC)

CARRIER Aircraft Color Markings
Per SR 2B 10-8-40

YORKTOWN

SARATOGA

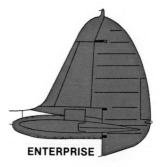
ENTERPRISE

WASP

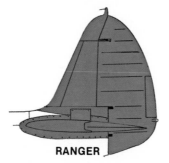
RANGER

LEXINGTON

Engine Cowl Markings - Each Section

	1st	2nd	3rd		4th	5th	6th

Right Wing

 2
 5
 8
 11
 14
 17

Leader

 1
 4
 7
 10
 13
 16

Left Wing

 3
 6
 9
 12
 15
 18

Wing Markings

7

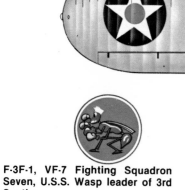

F-3F-1, VF-7 Fighting Squadron Seven, U.S.S. Wasp leader of 3rd Section.

7-F-7   U.S. NAVY

0262 F3F-1

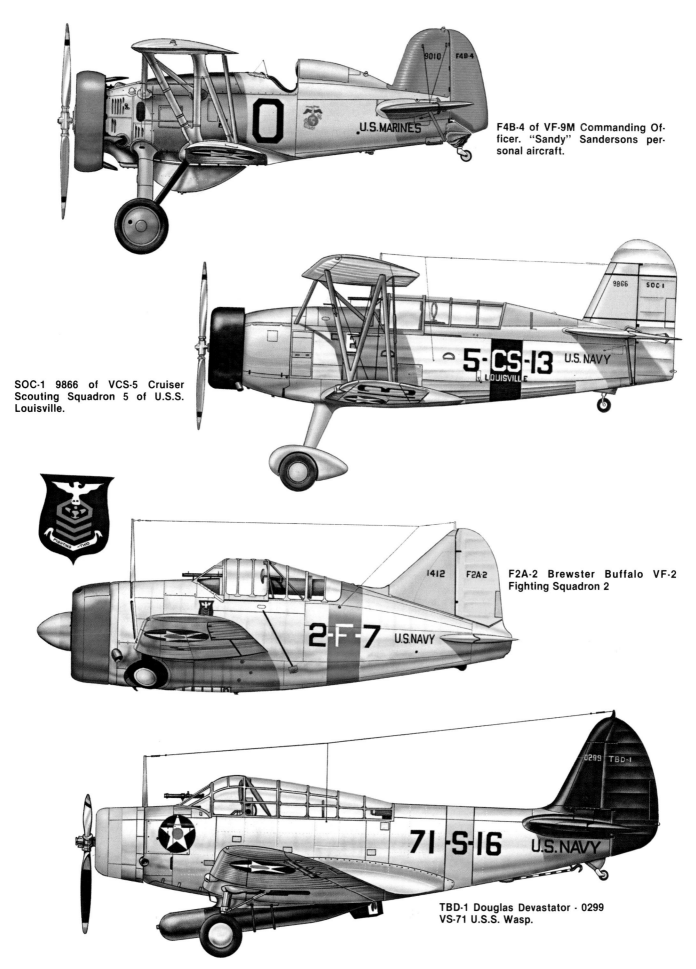

F4B-4 of VF-9M Commanding Officer. "Sandy" Sandersons personal aircraft.

SOC-1 9866 of VCS-5 Cruiser Scouting Squadron 5 of U.S.S. Louisville.

F2A-2 Brewster Buffalo VF-2 Fighting Squadron 2

TBD-1 Douglas Devastator - 0299 VS-71 U.S.S. Wasp.

Torpedo Squadron Three, from the USS SARATOGA CV-3, carries Insignia White tail (for Sara), Lemon Yellow fuselage band and wing chevron, glossy Orange-Yellow wing surfaces, over-sized "E", Lemon Yellow cowl, Black fuselage code 3-T-16, and VT-3 "Flying Dragon" squadron insignia. All applied per SR-2b. Aircraft is at NAS North Island in 1940. (W. Steed)

(Left) Line up of brand new SBD-1s for the Marine Corps on 12 September 1940. (Douglas Aircraft via H.S. Gann)

(Below Left) Marine Corps SBD-1 (1603) awaiting delivery to Marines at the Douglas factory, 12 September 1940. 1-MB-1 carried vertical tail stripes, Insignia Red fuselage band and wing chevrons, glossy Orange-Yellow wings, Aluminum varnished fuselage and Marine Corps insignia. Face of propeller is painted Flat Black as anti-reflection measure. Entire front half of cowling is painted Insignia Red on squadron commander's aircraft. (Douglas Aircraft via H.S. Gann)

SR-2B called for the individual aircraft number to be applied on the upper surface of the upper wing, in the center of the span in numerals of the largest practicable size. On low wing aircraft, monoplanes, and patrol planes, the number was to be painted on each outer wing panel, midway between the star insignia and the extremity of the outer wing panel. On patrol planes, this number was to be painted on the lower surface of the wing so as to be legible from the rear and low altitudes.

Model designation and Bureau number was applied to the airplane's rudder and vertical stabilizer respectively. In the case of a multiple rudder airplane, the model designation and Bureau number were to be applied to the outboard side of the vertical fin and rudder.

The rudder markings of United States Marine Corps, Naval Reserve, and shipboard utility (VJ) airplanes featured 3 vertical stripes of Blue, White and Red. The rudder surface aft of the rudder hinge was divided into three equal parts: Red at the trailing edge, White in the center, and Blue adjacent to the rudder hinge.

On Carrier Air Group Commander's aircraft, a diagonal band, 14 inches wide, of the same color as the distinguishing empennage painting of the carrier identification color, was applied around the fuselage. (See photo)

An individual squadron insignia was applied under the cockpit canopy, midway on the fuselage on some models, (see SB2U photo -VS-71), and below and forward of the pilot's cockpit on others.

Staff-Liaison and shore based planes applied the ship or station name on the airplane's fuselage, in a position usually occupied by the 2-T-1, etc., type fuselage coding.

SR-2Bs instructions regarding the empennage marking of Fleet patrol planes were as follows:

Patrol Wing One
Single Vertical Stripe on Elevators and Rudder.
    VP-11.....Insignia Red
    VP-12.....White
    VP-13.....True Blue
    VP-14.....Black

Patrol Wing Two
Double Vertical Stripe on Elevator and Rudder.
    VP-22.....Insignia Red
    VP-23.....White
    VP-24.....True Blue
    VP-25.....Black
    VP-26.....Willow Green
    VP-27.....Lemon Yellow

Patrol Wing Three
Single Horizontal Stripe on Elevator and Rudder.
    VP-31.....Insignia Red
    VP-32.....White
    VP-33.....True Blue
    VP-34.....Black

Patrol Wing Four
Double Horizontal Stripe on Elevator and Rudder.
    VP-41.....Insignia Red
    VP-42.....White
    VP-43.....True Blue
    VP-44.....Black

Patrol Wing Five
Solid, (Complete Empennage).
    VP-51.....Insignia Red
    VP-52.....White
    VP-53.....True Blue
    VP-54.....Black
    VP-55.....Willow Green
    VP-56.....Lemon Yellow

Patrol Wing Six
Checkered Pattern on Elevators and Rudders.
    VP-61.....Insignia Red
    VP-62.....White

Patrol Wing Seven
Double Vertical Strip on Elevator and Rudder.
    VP-71.....Insignia Red
    VP-72.....White

The Observation and Scouting squadrons serving the Fleet's battleships and cruisers came under the direction of SR-2B also. The aircraft assigned to the VO squadrons had their entire empennage painted in accordance with the instructions in SR-2B as follows:

VO-1 - Insignia Red	USS Arizona BB-39
	USS Nevada BB-36
	USS Pennsylvania BB-38
VO-2 - White	USS California BB-44
	USS Oklahoma BB-37
	USS Tennessee BB-43
VO-3 - True Blue	USS Idaho BB-42
	USS Mississippi BB-41
	USS New Mexico BB-40
VO-4 - Black	USS Colorado BB-45
	USS Maryland BB-46
	USS West Virginia BB-48
VO-5 - Lemon Yellow	USS Arkansas BB-33
	USS New York BB-34
	USS Texas BB-35

Black tailed OS2U-1 (1685) from the USS COLORADO BB-45. Ship's name under coding in Black and fuselage band in Insignia White. Cowling is also painted White. (A. Schoeni)

OS2U-1 from the USS MISSISSIPPI BB-41. Tail color is True Blue with Insignia White lettering. Squadron insignia, "Oswald the Lucky Rabbit", can be seen behind pilot's cockpit. Fuselage band, wing chevron and cowling are painted Insignia White. Note that both 4-O-4 and 3-O-4 have improperly shaped "4s" on fuselage and wings. Fuselage painted with Aluminum varnish per SR-2b. (A. Schoeni)

North American NJ-1 shows how Insignia Red wing bands, applied to instrument flying trainers, extended full chord of wing on underside of aircraft. This NJ-1 was based at NAS Pensacola in 1940. (Thomas C. Haywood)

Battleships normally carried 3 aircraft. The section colors of battleship planes were applied in the same manner as were those of carrier based machines.

All cruisers carried 4 plane units, except for CL-4 to CL-13 of the Omaha class, which carried only 2 planes. The section colors applied to the aircraft of the aforementioned 4 and 2 plane unit was marked with a vertical band in the proper color: -4 Insignia Red, -8 White, -12 True Blue, -16 Black and -20 Willow Green. This vertical band marking was painted on the engine cowling. The two plane unit's cowl markings actually followed the same pattern as carrier and battleship assigned aircraft, i.e. the first airplane in the section had the entire frontal section of the cowling painted, and the 2nd airplane only had the top half of its cowling finished. The difference was that while aircraft number 3 in a carrier based squadron would normally have the bottom half of it's cowling painted Red, aircraft number 3 of a 2 plane cruiser unit would have it's entire cowling painted White. (see chart)

Cruiser based scouting squadrons came under SR-2B, when a set of tail markings were detailed on page 11 of the original document. The markings were to be applied to the elevators and rudder of each aircraft involved in shipboard VCS operations.

The assignments were as follows:

VCS-2 — True Blue - Double Horizontal Stripe

VCS-3 — Insignia Red - Double Horizontal Stripe
    USS Concord CL-10
    USS Cincinnati, CL-6
    USS Milwaukee CL-5
    USS Omaha CL-4
    USS Trenton CL-11

VCS-4 — True Blue - Single Horizontal Stripe
    USS Northhampton CA-26
    USS Houston CA-30
    USS Pensacola CA-24
    USS Salt Lake City CA-25

VCS-5 — Lemon Yellow - Single Horizontal Stripe
    USS Chicago CA-29
    USS Chester CA-27
    USS Louisville CA-28
    USS Portland CA-33

VCS-6 — Black - Single Horizontal Stripe
    USS Minneapolis CA-36
    USS Astoria CA-34
    USS New Orleans CA-32
    USS San Francisco CA-38

VCS-7 — Willow Green - Single Horizontal Stripe
    USS Quincy CA-39
    USS Tuscaloosa CA-37

    USS Wichita CA-45
    USS Vincennes CA-44

VCS-8 — Black - Double Horizontal Stripe
    USS Philadelhia CL-41
    USS Brooklyn CL-40
    USS Nashville CL-43
    USS Savannah CL-42

VCS-9 — Willow Green - Double Horizontal Stripe
    USS Honolulu CL-48
    USS Boise CL-47
    USS St. Louis CL-49
    USS Phoenix CL-46

USS Raleigh	CL-7	Insignia Blue - Double Horizontal Stripe
USS Detroit	CL-8	Insignia Blue - Double Horizontal Stripe
USS Richmond	CL-9	Insignia Red - Double Horizontal Stripe

The Navy's Three shore based utility squadrons were assigned tail colors in SR-2B. The order called for the entire empennage to be painted as follows:
    VJ-1...Willow Green
    VJ-2...Lemon Yellow
    VJ-3...Aluminum

Instrument flying airplanes, additional to the normal squadron compliment, were to be painted with two Red fore and aft stripes, three feet wide, on the upper surfaces of the upper wings and lower surfaces of the lower wings, with a Red band, three feet wide, around the fuselage forward of the horizontal stabilizer.

An interesting, and perhaps little known, marking specified in SR-2B, concerned the proper method of wing strut numbering applied to pre-WW II

Squadron Insignia Examples
Paintings by Tom Doll

VT-2
1939

VT-5
1938

VT-6
1939

VT-27
1945

VF-6B
1932

VF-6
1938

VF-10
1942

VMF-214
1944

VF-4
1939

VMF-323
1944

VMF-111
1941

VP-31
1939

πρῶτοι ἔπλμεν

VB-5B
1935

VMTB-232
1945

VS-3
1937

VS-2
1939

VS-42
1943

VS-71
1940

VO-3
1941

VMO-251
1942

VJ-1B
1930

VMJ-2
1941

USN aircraft. All wing struts were to be numbered to indicate their position on the airplane. The strut number was to be applied one inch from the lower end of the strut, and a corresponding number applied on the lower wing or fuselage close to the lower strut fitting. The figures were to be 1 inch in height. The front outermost strut on the right of the pilot was to be numbered 1 and the remaining front struts were marked in order from right to left with consecutive odd numbers. The right rear outermost strut received the number 2, while the remaining rear struts from right to left were marked with consecutive even numbers.

In the pre-WW II time period, almost all US Navy aircraft painting was accomplished at the seven overhaul facilities set up at the following locations:

NAS San Diego, California	Code Letters - SD
NAS Norfolk, Virginia	Code Letters - NOR
Naval Aircraft Factory	Code Letters - NAF
NAS Pensacola, Florida	Code Letters - PEN
NAS Pearl Harbor, Territory of Hawaii	Code Letters - PH
NAS Seattle, Washington	Code Letters - SE

The material used to paint pre-WW II Navy airplanes was specified in a series of documents originally issued prior to 1940, and discussed in the preceeding chapter. Clear varnish, pigmented with aluminum powder, was still being used as the basic exterior coating. All additional color added to the airplane was accomplished with the use of lacquer.

After the painting of each Navy aircraft, a set of letters and figures were applied to the undersurfaces of the plane's fuselage, wings and control surfaces. This code designated the number of coats applied to the aircraft, the materials used, the date of application and the overhaul facility where the airplane was painted. These letters and figures were to be applied with Black paint and were to be 1/2 inch in height. A typical example of this code is as follows:

4-2D12d 8-15-40 SD-	Indicated 4 clear and 2 Aluminum pigmented coats of D12d dope, finished 15 August 1940 at NAS San Diego.
4D12d 3D13c 8-15-40 NAF-	Indicates 4 clear coats of D12d and 3 coats of D13c (Yellow) dope, finished 15 August 1940 at the Naval Aircraft Factory

The painting of US Naval aircraft in the bright hues listed in SR-2B, was destined to come to an end within a few short months after the instructions were issued. The Neutrality Patrol continued into late 1940, and due to the increased possibility of contact with the ''enemy'', it was decided by the Bureau that a low-visibility paint scheme should be adopted by Fleet aircraft to lessen the chance of giving visual aid to the opposition.

On 30 December 1940, a directive was put forth by BuAer, which stated

Consolidated PBY-1 from NAS Squantum, Massachusetts, in 1941. Top half of engine cowlings painted True Blue. 4-J-8 and hull stripe are Black. (USN/National Archives)

Curtiss SOC-4 based at Port Angeles, Washington in 1939. Noteworthy is the USCG insignia on fuselage, absence of national insignia on top surface of wing and unique Coast Guard rudder paint scheme. Top of wing is glossy Orange-Yellow, top third of rudder is Insignia Blue with Insignia Red and White vertical stripes. Balance of plane is Aluminum varnish. Noted aviation photographer Gordon S. Williams took this picture of photo plane from the rear seat of V 173. (G.S. Williams collection via W.T. Larkins)

that the exterior surfaces of all ship based aircraft would be painted *Non-specular Light Gray. The exterior surfaces of Fleet patrol aircraft would be painted NS Blue Gray on surfaces viewed from above, and NS Light Gray on all surfaces viewed from below. Even though the directive AER-E-25-FZ, F-39-5 (00261), was issued in December, the actual changeover did not really get under way until well into 1941.

Between the time of the December order and the follow-up directive AER-3-25-HY, F-39-5, F-39-1 (010282) of 26 February 1941, there appears to be a period of time when airplanes painted in the overall NS Light Gray scheme would have little or no markings. To date, the only known examples of this happening are illustrated on the pages of this book. This occurrence was probably very rare, as the difference between the 30 December 1940 directive, and the 26 February 1941 letter is so short a time period, most commands very likely did not even have the paint with which to effect the change. The 26 February directive cleared up the mystery and the change-over began to take place within the Fleet.

Hereafter the letters NS will designate the term Non-Specular.

V-202 from Biloxi, Mississippi in 1941. Orange-Yellow on top of wing extended over leading edge of wing as far as float strut. Letters "USCG" were painted on the undersides of both wings in Black paint. Serial number "V202" painted on underside of hull in Black also. J4F-1 had wing span of 40' and it's length was 31' 1". Of note is the unit cost, $75,526.00. (USCG)

Grumman J4F-1 from Port Angeles during 1941. (G.S. Williams)

Transitional period...from December 1940 to February 1941, there was no document covering markings for the overall Light Grey paint scheme. This photo, taken at NAS North Island, shows Vought SB2Us in the overall Grey scheme without full markings. The only markings visible are on the vertical fin and rudder. Base personnel, not knowing for sure which markings to apply to the overall Light Grey scheme, apparently reapplied the Bureau Number and model designation in the old style so at least that vital bit of data would be on the airplane. The partially folded wings of Douglas TBD-1s can be seen in the foreground of this photo. The wing nearest the camera has the hi-visibility Orange-Yellow top wing surfaces while the other TBDs have the overall Light Grey paint. (USN/National Archives)

More transitional period...VF-42 F4F-3 at Chambers Field, NAS Norfolk in March 1941. Still in the pre-WW II paint scheme, this F4F carries White fuselage coding in preparation for the overall Light Grey scheme. Fuselage coding is 42-F-18, BuNo. 2537. (Capt. W.E. Scarborough, USN, Ret.)

With the adoption of the overall NS Light Gray scheme, all fuselage coding, wing numerals, cowling numbers, model designations and Bureau number markings, was accomplished by the application of NS Insignia White paint. The manner of applying fuselage codes remained as they had been prior to the changeover to the Gray scheme, i.e., 2-T-1, etc. This time however, all fuselage codes were to be only 12 inches in height on all aircraft regardless of type. Twelve inch numerals were positioned on the wings of monoplanes at a point outboard of the aircraft's fuselage, equal to one-half the the width of the fuselage. Individual airplane numbers were painted on the forward portion of the engine cowling in four inch figures. The airplane's model designation was painted on the rudder (both sides) in one-inch figures, and the word "NAVY" or "MARINES" and the Bureau number directly underneath the branch of service lettering appeared on the plane's vertical stabilizer, also in one-inch figures.

The national insignia was added to the aft fuselage between the trailing edge of the wing and the leading edge of the horizontal stabilizer. At this same time, the top (starboard) and bottom (port) wing national insignia was removed, leaving one insignia in the top port position and one insignia in the bottom starboard position.

Patrol plane fuselage codes were applied with NS Black paint. These codes, i.e., 22-P-7, were located on each side of the seaplane's bow, aft of the US national insignia.

Aircraft that were based on ships other than aircraft carriers, battleships and cruisers, had the ship's name printed on the fuselage below the squadron class and plane number designation.

When aircraft were not assigned to regularly organized squadrons, the name of the ship to which the plane was attached was painted on the fuselage in the position usually occupied by the markings of the squadron, immediately forward of the natioal insignia. For patrol planes in this category, this marking was applied aft of the bow national insignia. For identification pur-

poses, the serial number assigned to each airplane by the ship was painted immediately following the name of the ship. For example, "USS RANGER -3".

Instrument flying aircraft, additional to the normal flying complement, were painted with two Red fore and aft stripes, three feet wide on the upper surface of the upper wing and the lower surface of the lower wing, with a Red band three feet wide around the fuselage forward of the horizontal stabilizer.

Propeller blades were painted on both sides with non-specular colors as follows:

Vertically from the tip to four inches from the tip - Insignia Red.

Four inches to eight inches from tip - Orange-Yellow.

Eight inches from tip to twelve inches from tip - Insignia Blue.

The remaining blade area, front and back, was painted either NS Black or Insignia Blue. The application of paint to this area was not necessary if the propeller was delivered with this surface finished in anodic coating dyed Black or Dark Blue. Propellers on patrol planes did not have to have the warning stripes on the tips if the locations of the propeller did not present a hazard to personnel. They did, however, have to have the blades painted Blue or Black.

Group Commanders' aircraft had the letters "COMMANDER (name of ship) GROUP" painted in letters 4'' in height horizontally on each side of the fuselage.

Individual squadron insignia could be applied on each side of the fuselage, forward of the squadron numbers on land and seaplanes, and forward of the tail surfaces on the hulls of patrol planes, provided it did not interfere with other specified markings. The size of squadron insignia was not to exceed an area bound by a 6'' square. The common practice of squadron insignia applicaton was to position the insignia in an area just below and forward of the cockpit canopy windshield on the side of the airplane's fuselage.

Excellent example of overall Light Grey scheme on Douglas SBD-3 (4532). Bureau Number and model designation are Insignia White one inch figures. National insignia star appeared on top left wing and bottom right wing only, while fuselage star appeared as shown on aft fuselage. (Douglas Aircraft via B. Donato)

VMSB-131 SB2U-3 shows to advantage the 12 inch Insignia White fuselage coding as applied to Marine Corps aircraft per the painting directive issued 26 February 1941. VMSB-131 was formerly VMS-1 before the 1 July 1941 squadron designation changes. (USMC)

The Gunnery E, when used, was normally placed on the fuselage side approxmately 8 to 10 inches below the cockpit canopy. This figure was not to exceed 3'' in height.

On Marine Corps airplanes, the Marine Corps insignia was eliminated, as were the vertical Red, White and Blue rudder stripes.

1941

Many important changes took place in 1941. In July, the 1st and 2nd Marine Aircraft Wings were commissioned. Within these wings, there were two Marine Air Groups, one to each wing. MAG-11 was at Quantico, Virginia, and MAG-21 was officially at San Diego, but most of the group was located on the island of Oahu in Hawaii. At the time of the organization of the two MAWs, Marine Corps squadrons were redesignated, and the re-numbered were as follows:

VMF-1	to	VMF-111
VMS-1	to	VMSB-131
VMB-1	to	VMSB-132
VMO-1	to	VMO-151
VMS-3	to	VMS-3
VMF-2	to	VMF-211
VMS-2	to	VMSB-231
VMB-2	to	VMSB-232
VMJ-2	to	VMJ-252

The new system of squadron identification called for the first numeral of the designation to represent the MAW to which the squadron belonged, and the second number indicated the MAG to which the squadron belonged, which the last number in the designation identified the squadron itself.

Marine Corps airplanes prior to the redesignation carried the fuselage codes 2-S-16, etc., however, after the 1 July 1941 change, they carried fuselage coding 231-MB-16, etc.

Also, in 1941, the Navy's patrol squadrons were re-organized. Not all VP squadrons were re-numbered, but several changes are evident in the following list.*

VP-23 to VP-11	PBY-1	Kaneohe, Hawaii
VP-24 to VP-12	PBY-1	Kaneohe, Hawaii
VP-13	PBY-4	TTU-Pacific (New Squadron)
	PBY-5	
VP-14 to VP-14	PBY-5	Kaneohe, Hawaii
VP-11 to VP-21	PBY-3	Pearl Harbor, Hawaii
VP-22 to VP-22	PBY-3	Pearl Harbor, Hawaii
VP-25 to VP-23	PBY-2	Pearl Harbor, Hawaii
VP-12 to VP-24	PBY-5	Pearl Harbor, Hawaii
VP-31 to VP-31	PBY-5	Coco Solo and San Juan
VP-33 to VP-32	PBY-3	Coco Solo
VP-41 to VP-41	PBY-5	Alaska
VP-42 to VP-42	PBY-5	Alaska
VP-43	PBY-5	Alaska (New Squadron)
VP-44	PBY-5	Alaska (New Squadron)
VP-54 to VP-51	PBY-5	Norfolk and Bermuda
VP-32 to VP-52	PBY-5	Norfolk
VP-51 to VP-71	PBY-5	Support Force
VP-52 to VP-72	PBY-5	Support Force

US NAVY AIRCRAFT 1921-1941 by William T. Larkins 1961 Aviation History Publications Concord, California.

VF-71 (WASP) F4F-3 in overall Light Grey paint, early 1941. Wing insignia was not to exceed 60 inches in diameter or intrude upon the aileron. (Capt. W.E. Scarborough, USN, Ret.)

F4F-3s from either a Navy or Marine squadron are seen during joint Army/Navy war exercises in Southern Louisiana in 1941. Large White crosses identified "White" forces. "Red" forces carried Red crosses on their aircraft. (USN/National Archives)

VB-8 SBC-4 is escorted by VMF-111 F4F-3s during 1941 exercises. Compare size and location of these Red crosses with White crosses on aircraft of the White forces. SBC-4 had large Red cross painted on center section of top wing and is just visible on the leading edge of the wing. (Smithsonian Institution)

Alaska based VP-42 PBY-5 carries Non-specular Blue Grey top surfaces with Non-specular Light Grey undersurfaces. This scheme, adopted in early 1941 for VP aircraft, would, before the end of 1941, become standard on all USN carrier based aircraft. Hull code, 42-P-3, was applied with Non-specular Black paint. Figures were 12 inches high. (USN/National Archives)

SBD-3, belonging to Cdr. Howard Young, Commander Enterprise Air Group, displays carrier plane paint scheme directed by the Bureau on 13 October 1941. Top surface color was Non-specular Blue Grey with Non-specular Light Grey undersides. The legend "COMMANDER ENTERPRISE GROUP" is barely visible directly forward of fuselage national insignia star. This lettering was 4 inches high and applied with Non-specular Black paint. Letters "CEG" also appear on top of SBD's wing near non-skid walkway. (USN via H.S. Gann)

VP-53 to VP-73	PBY-5	Support Force
VP-55 and		
VP-56 to VP-74	PBM-1	VP-55 & 56 merged to form VP-74
VP-43 to VP-81	PBY-5	Support Force
VP-44 to VP-82	PBY-5	Support Force
VP-83	PBY-5A	Organized 9/15/41 at Norfolk
VP-84	PBY-5A	Organized 10/1/41 at Norfolk
VP-91	PBY-5A	New at Quonset Point
VP-92	PBY-5A	New at Quonset Point
VP-93	PBY-5A	New at Quonset Point
VP-94	PBY-5A	New at Quonset Point
VP-21 to VP-101	PBY-4	Cavite, Phillippine Islands
VP-26 to VP-102	PBY-4	Cavite, Phillippine Islands

On 1 October 1941, the Secretary of the Navy directed that US Navy aircraft were to carry names in addition to their letter-number designations. Thus, for the general public, fighting planes of the US Navy took on names that were somewhat belligerent in nature.*

Grumman F4F . . . . Wildcat
Brewster F2A . . . . Buffalo
Vought-Sikorsky F4U . . . . Corsair
Consolidated PBY . . . . Catalina
Martin PBM . . . . Mariner
Martin XPB2M . . . . Mars

Vought OS2U-1 (1697) from VO-1 on board the USS ARIZONA BB-39 in late 1941. Battleship and Cruiser aircraft were painted the same as carrier based aircraft at that time. Fuselage code was 12 inches high with the White letters "ARIZONA", a hold-over from the overall Light Grey scheme, in 3 inch figures. (USN/National Archives)

Consolidated PB2Y . . . . Coronado
Boeing PBB . . . . Sea Ranger
Douglas TBD . . . . Devastator
Grumman TBF . . . . Avenger
Brewster SB2A . . . . Buccaneer
Curtiss SB2C . . . . Helldiver
Douglas SBD . . . . Dauntless
Vought-Sikorsky SB2U . . . . . . Vindicator
Curtiss SO3C . . . . Seagull
Vought-Sikorsky OS2U . . . . . . Kingfisher

United States Naval Aviation continued it's expansion, if not by leaps and bounds then, at least, by inches and feet.

The next change to occur relative to USN camouflage, took place on 13

This list appeared on page 232 of the January 1942 Special Issue devoted to US Naval Aviation of FLYING AND POPULAR AVIATION. The issue went to press before the attack on Pearl Harbor and appeared on the newsstands during the week of 8 December 1941.

Patrol Squadron 11 PBY-5 (11-P-12) behind cinder pile of what used to be a PBY at NAS Kaneohe, Hawaii. Photo was taken on 8 December 1941. Close examination of intact PBY-5 reveals a very unusual paint scheme for this time period. Six varying shades of color are visible especially on the aft fuselage near the PBY's tail section. This scheme is most likely experimental and could have been the forerunner of the tri-color camouflage scheme adopted in February 1943. Any comment, as of this writing, is wholly theoretical as documentation covering this paint application has yet to be found. Keeping this

October 1941, with the issuing of BuAer directive Aer-E-2571-DMC, F39-5, VV, FF12, 063183.

This directive called for all carrier and ship based aircraft to be painted the same as patrol planes; which was NS Light Gray on the bottom surfaces, and on surfaces viewed from above, NS Blue Gray. The line of demarcation between the two colors was to be an irregular, wavy line with one color blending into the other color so as to avoid a sharp, definite line between the top surface color and the bottom surface color. This blended line was interpreted in various ways depending upon the painter. Examples of the soft blended line show up in period photographs as do examples of a not-so soft blended line of demarcation. In reality it probably didn't make that much difference.

Specific instructions regarding aircraft with upward folding wings were also issued. Aircraft that had wings that folded in such a manner that exposed the undersurfaces to view from above were to have these exposed parts painted with the NS Blue Gray color. Aircraft covered by this order were the Douglas TBD-1 and the Vought SB2U series.

With the adoption of the Blue Gray paint scheme, the color of the fuselage codes as well as all the other letters and numbers eventually were changed to NS Black. A few squadrons continued the use of White paint for their mark-

in mind, the authors speculate that a color very similar to Non-specular Sea Blue was used on the top surfaces of the aircraft. Various shades of Blue Grey, light, very light, etc., on through to a bottom color of Non-specular Light Grey completed the scheme. Proof of this camouflage paint application, to date, exists only in this photograph. Official Bureau of Aeronautics documentation does not cover experimental paint schemes during this time period. (USN/National Archives va R.P. Gill)

The positioning of the small US national insignia star is very far forward on the fuselage of this Douglas SBD scout bomber. Inside surface of dive flaps were painted glossy Insignia Red. (USN via H.S. Gann)

Goodyear's 147' training blimp displays 54" Insignia Blue branch of service and model designation marking on Aluminum painted envelope. Tail stripes are Insignia Red, White and Blue. The L ships were powered by two Warner engines, giving them a top speed of 60 mph. (Goodyear Tire & Rubber Co.)

ings well into the first few months of 1942, but overall the use of Black in the application of markings became standard practice.

The reference used in determining the color of fuselage codes, etc., was the directive issued on 26 February 1941. Letters and numerals were to be of the lowest contrast to the background color. White on Light Gray and Black on Blue Gray.

All other markings stayed the same as originally directed by the 26 February letter. Mention of a readily-removable NS Black, night camouflage paint for use on naval aircraft was made in the 13 October directive. This paint was developed at the Naval Research Laboratory in Anacostia, D.C. Service tests were made by the Fleet, but photographic examples have yet to turn up as of this writing. A NS Light Gray finish for camouflaging rubber tires was also developed at the same time.

A short, one page directive, issued on 26 December 1941, called for all shore based aircraft except training types to be painted in the same manner as all carrier and ship based aircraft. This letter was coded Aer-E-257SGE, F39-5, VV, FF12, 083718.

Douglas SBD-3 reflects markings per the directive issued on 5 January 1942. Seven Insignia Red and six Insignia White horizontal tail stripes were added to aid visual identification of USN aircraft. The national insignia was placed on the top surface of the starboard wing and on the underside of the port wing. The basic camouflage remained Non-specular Blue Grey topside and Non-specular Light Grey underside. (USN/National Archives)

A Fighting Six F4F-3 receives large diameter national insignia approved by the Bureau on 17 January 1942. This insignia was not to exceed 50" in diameter and in the 17 January letter, the Bureau stated their disapproval of the wing national insignia being applied from leading edge to trailing edge, but, as evidenced by the F4F in the background, this order was not always followed. (USN/National Archives)

SBD-3 prepares for take-off from ENTERPRISE in early 1942. Huge national insignia shows well on underside of wing and Black rubber coated propeller spinner gleams in the early morning sunlight. (USN/National archives)

1942

After the entry of the United States into World War II, markings on US Navy, Marine Corps and Coast Guard aircraft underwent a rather startling change. A two page directive, Aer-E-2571-BP, F39-5, VV, FF12, 001085, issued by the Bureau on 5 January 1942, directed that the following changes in markings be effected. The US national insignia was to be placed on the upper side of the upper wing and the underside of the lower wing on both right and left wings. The insignias were to be of the maximum diameter possible without overflowing onto the aileron. They were to be placed inboard from the wing tip approximately 1/3 of the distance from wing tip to fuselage. The fuselage insignia was to be 24 inches in diameter. If the 24 inch diameter insignia could not be applied in accordance with the then existing instructions, then the point of application could be moved forward on the fuselage as necessary. This last notation most likely accounts for the variations in the application of the fuselage insignia, often in evidence in photographs from this

Deck scene aboard the USS ENTERPRISE CV-6 shortly after the Marcus Island raid of 4 March 1942. Many variations in markings are visible. (USN/National Archives)

time period.

Vertical rudders were to be striped horizontally on both sides with 13 alternate Red and White stripes parallel to the longitudinal axis of the airplane. The location of the stripes was determined by dividing the distance between the highest and lowest points on the rudder into thirteen equal parts, there were supposed to be 7 Red and 6 White stripes. Balanced portions of rudders which extended into the fin were to be finished in the same color as the fin surfaces. This section of the directive was subject to personal interpretation as evidenced in the accompanying photographs. All markings were to be Non-Specular in finish.

All other markings, i.e., lettering, prop tips, etc., remained the same as did the basic camouflage scheme.

This changes applied to all Fleet aircraft but not to primary or advanced training aircraft.

A little more than one week later, on 14 January, the Bureau issued a short one page directive Aer-E-2571-MVS, F39-5 (004159), stating that the use of a Non-Specular Temporary Black paint was authorized for temporary night use over the day camouflage scheme. This paint would be used at the discretion of the force commander, and would be applied by spraying in the usual manner prescribed, and it would be readily removable with soap and water

Early in WW II small Japanese flags began to make their appearance on the fuselages of USN/USMC aircraft as a symbol of victory over the enemy. This marking on LCdr Lance Massey's VT-6 TBD-1. Sinking ship superimposed on flag, was one of the earliest examples. (USN/National Archives)

VP-22 PBY-3 preparing for take-off from Pearl Harbor for an anti-sub patrol around the islands, February 1942. Not often seen aft location of US national insignia is noteworthy. Good view of full chord national insignia on top of wing. (USN/National Archives)

Deck of either SARATOGA CV-3 or LEXINGTON CV-2 sometime in early 1942. SBD in center of photograph has individual aircraft number 12 applied to top of vertical fin. This practice does not appear common at this stage of war. Of note is the absence of the national insignia from the top right-hand wing surface. This was to be applied along with the tail stripes but obviously the actual work failed to get done. White LSO stripe is visible on vertical fin. (USN)

Grumman F4F-3P (2524) at Norfolk on 7 May 1942. Squadron is VGF-27 which went on to become VF-27 on 1 March 1943. By this point in 1942, most fuselage coding was applied with Non-specular Black paint. (USN/National Archives via D. Bruce Van Alstine)

Vought OS2U-2 of Inshore Patrol Squadron Two at Darrell's Island, Bermuda, March 1942. Use of tail stripes with overall Light Grey scheme is unusual at this late date. (USN/National Archives via D. Bruce Van Alstine)

US Navy SNV-1s in flight during early 1942. Vultee "Vibrators" with USN Bureau Numbers and model designation and US Army Air Corps paint scheme (Medium Blue fuselage, Yellow wings and tail) along with USAAC style tail marking (Blue vertical bar) and USAAC identification legend stenciled in White just forward of the cockpit, make these planes an interesting subject for markings buffs and scale modellers. Numbers "1389" on lower fin is former Army identification number. USN Bureau Numbers are 03059 and 03060. A third SNV-1 is almost totally hidden behind 03059. (Spence Air Photos)

for day missions.

It appears at this writing, that carrier aircraft used this temporary Black paint rarely, if at all. However, VP-12, the originator of the term "Black Cat" for its night prowling squadron, did use the NS Black paint as did the many other patrol squadrons that served in this role. VP-12's PBY-5A's went to overall NS Black in early December 1942.

On this same day, 14 January, a letter from the Inspector of Naval Aircraft at Douglas-El Segundo arrived at the Bureau requesting approval to apply the fuselage insignia in a diameter of 50 inches. Also the INA wanted to know if the wing insignia should be applied from the leading edge to the trailing edge of the wing. On 17 January, the Bureau approved the 50 inch fuselage insignia in BUAER letter Aer-E-2571-JWM-1478. A footnote to this letter indicated that the Bureau did not approve the application of the wing insignia from the leading edge to the trailing edge, but they did OK the application of the insignia from the leading edge to the aileron cutout. On Fleet aircraft carriers, this wing insignia was applied at the whim of the plane captain as shown in photographs. At sea, time was of vital importance, and as far as the proper application of such things as wing insignia was concerned, if insignia was put on properly, then fine, but if applied slightly out-of-round, or too oversized, tough luck.

On 6 February 1942, the Bureau issued a 9 page directive, Aer-E-2571-MVS, F39-5, F39-1, 012076, designed to put all the recent markings changes under one document for purposes of uniformity. The basic camouflage scheme remained Blue Gray from above and Light Gray from below. Prop tips stayed in the 3 color band style, while squadron ID markings remained as before, 2-T-1, etc. The color of the squadron markings remained either Black

or White, depending on the background to which they were applied. White on Light Gray and Black on Blue Gray. Letters and numerals applied to tail surfaces, however, were to be Black. Model designation and service markings on the fin and rudder stayed as before. Group Commanders' aircraft had the number of the carrier air group painted in letters four inches in height horizontally on each side of the fuselage. For example, Lexington Group Commanders plane was marked thus, "2".

The 6 February directive was basically an affirmation of what had been in effect since the change-over from the colorful high visibility markings of early 1941. The main changes in markings listed in this directive were:
(1) Two more national insignia were added to the wing surfaces.
(2) The size of the national insignia on the wings and fuselage were expanded to the maximum size possible within reasonable limits.
(3) Rudder stripes were added.
(4) Stripes on instrument flying planes were changed from Red to Light Green.
(5) Aircraft regularly attached to squadrons, but based on surface vessels other than aircraft carriers, were to be marked only with the squadron number. The name of the ship was to be omitted.

The temporary night camouflage was once again called out in this directive as well as a rubber paint for camouflaging tires and de-icer boots.

It should be noted that advanced training aircraft were to be painted in accordance with the order issued on 26 March 1942. SR-15d stated that these types were to have the familiar Glossy Orange-Yellow top wing surfaces with the remainder of the aircraft to be painted Glossy Aircraft Gray.

Marine Corps F4F-4 on Palmyra Island illustrates changes brought about by introduction of ALNAV Dispatch 062230 of 15 May 1942. Horizontal Red and White tail stripes have been removed as well as the Red disc from the center of the national insignia star. Top surface color is Non-specular Blue Grey. (USMC)

Brewster SB2A-2s show top wing surface location of US national insignia for this type of aircraft. (Mid-1942 photo by Jesse E. Hartman Via W.T. Larkins Collection)

Example of oversized national insignia sans Red disc on this Vought OS2U-3 Kingfisher in mid-1942. (USMC via R.P. Gill)

Douglas SBD-4s on the production line on 1 January 1943. Dauntlesses are primed and will soon receive Non-specuar Blue Grey and Light Grey paint. (Douglas Aircraft via H.S. Gann)

SBD-4 fuselages after painting, 1 January 1943. (Douglas Aircraft via H.S. Gann)

SBD-4s illustrate 1 inch Bureau Number, branch of service and model designation stenciling as applied to US Navy, Marine Corps and Coast Guard camouflaged aircraft during World War II. (Douglas Aircraft via H.S. Gann)

Coast Guard Kingfisher patrols over a convoy in the Atlantic during 1942. Entire underside of OS2U is painted Non-specular Light Grey. (USCG)

Wear and tear of sea duty is apparent on this Curtiss SOC Seagull. SOCs equipped many heavy cruisers during WW II. (USN/National Archives)

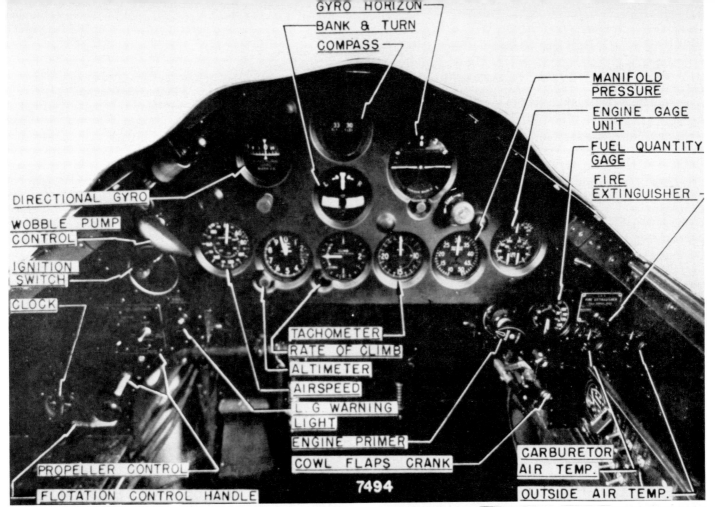

GYRO HORIZON
BANK & TURN
COMPASS

MANIFOLD PRESSURE
ENGINE GAGE UNIT
FUEL QUANTITY GAGE
FIRE EXTINGUISHER

DIRECTIONAL GYRO
WOBBLE PUMP CONTROL
IGNITION SWITCH
CLOCK

TACHOMETER
RATE OF CLIMB
ALTIMETER
AIRSPEED
L G WARNING LIGHT
ENGINE PRIMER
COWL FLAPS CRANK

CARBURETOR AIR TEMP.

PROPELLER CONTROL
FLOTATION CONTROL HANDLE

OUTSIDE AIR TEMP.

7494

Interior view of Grumman F4F-3 Wildcat illustrate use of Interior Green primer on bulkheads and pilot's seat. Instrument Black paint was used on instrument panel. (USN/Photo Lab-Pensacola)

AMMUNITION ROUNDS COUNTER
FLAP CONTROL
FUEL TANK SELECTOR VALVE
RUD. TAB CONTROL
AIL. TAB CONTROL
MIXTURE
SUPERCHARGER CONTROL
ELEV. TAB CONTROL
MICROPHONE SWITCH
THROTTLE
BOMB CONTROL
TAIL WHEEL LOCK

Port side. (USN/Photo Lab-Pensacola)

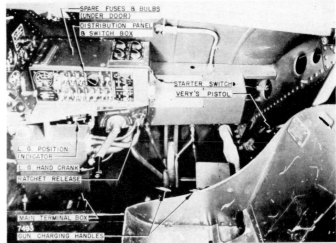

SPARE FUSES & BULBS (UNDER DOOR)
DISTRIBUTION PANEL & SWITCH BOX
STARTER SWITCH
VERY'S PISTOL
L.G. POSITION INDICATOR
L G HAND CRANK RATCHET RELEASE
MAIN TERMINAL BOX
7493
GUN CHARGING HANDLES

Starboard side. (USN/Photo Lab-Pensacola)

Primary trainers were painted overall Glossy Orange-Yellow except for the landing gear or float, which was to be finished in Glossy Aircraft Gray. Utility types were to be finished the same as service types.

According to SR-15d, the cockpit interiors of service airplanes were to be finished in dull Dark Green to match the Army-Navy color standard. Flying boat interiors were at the discretion of the contractors. Paragraph M-6a of SR-15d states that "Contractors shall submit a proposal for the interior finish scheme for flying boats, together with an inboard profile drawing with the color scheme indicated thereon."

Other personnel spaces (flying boats) were to be, in general, finished in Semi-Gloss pastel Green or Blue. The exact shades were subject to Bureau approval.

The inside surfaces of diving brakes were to be painted Insignia Red.

US Navy, Marine Corps and Coast Guard planes now sported the most colorful and visual low visibility camouflage paint scheme of any nation then engaged in World War II. US Coast Guard aircraft adopted the same basic camouflage scheme as the aircraft of the Navy and Marines. The Coast Guard began operating as part of the Navy through an Executive Order from

the President of the United States dated 1 November 1941. The Coast Guard continued to operate as part of the Navy until 28 December 1945. On that date, another Presidential directive returned the Coast Guard to the US Treasury Department.

One major battle, (Coral Sea 4 to 8 May 1942), and several lesser engagements, were fought by Navy planes in this very colorful markings scheme. By the beginning of May '42, thoughts of abandoning the markings then in use became more prevalent among the powers-that-be in the Bureau. Many reports of too much Red on our airplanes, which could be a source of confusion during high speed manuevering; (the Japanese national insignia was and still is a Red disc), coupled with the reports that our aircraft markings were too visual brought about a marking change on 15 May. ALN Dispatch 062230 called for the removal of the Red and White rudder stripes as well as the removal of the Red disc from our national insignia. National insignia size was reduced to the size outlined in the 26 February 1941 directive. The diameter of the circumscribed circle was to be equal to the distance between the leading edge of the aileron and the leading edge of the wing, provided that the distance was not in excess of 60 inches. The diameter of the circumscribed circle on the fuselage was called out as no more than 24 inches in the 26 Febuary 1941 directive, but after the elimination of the Red markings in mid-May, the fuselage insignia size varied; some photos show insignia of large size but very few of only 24 inches in diameter. All of the markings, and the basic camouflage color scheme, remained the same after the removal of the rudder stripes etc.

No other exterior changes took place during the remainder of 1942. On 22 December, a directive standardizing the interior color of aircraft was issued. Aer-E-2574-MVS, F38-2 called out Interior Green for all US Naval aircraft.

The next exterior color change came about with the issuing of Specification SR-2c on 5 January 1943. The effective date of SR-2c was 5 January 1943. The effective date of SR-2c was 1 February of the same year.

The new scheme outlined in SR-2c called out that:

All horizontal airfoil surfaces viewed from above should be finished in Semi-Gloss Sea Blue color.

All horizontal airfoil surfaces viewed from below should be finished in the NS Insignia White color.

The leading edge of the wing was to be countershaded between the two colors, using NS Insignia White and NS Sea Blue. The NS Sea Blue should extend back on the top of the wing surface approximately 5% of the wing chord.

When aircraft had wings that folded, so as to expose under-surfaces to view from above, these visible surfaces were to be painted NS Intermediate Blue.

Upper hull or fuselage surfaces extending down to a line, the tangent to which is approximately sixty degrees from the horizontal, was to be painted NS Sea Blue. (i.e. upper points of tangency).

Lower hull or fuselage surfaces extending up the side to a line, the tangent to which at any point is not more than thirty degrees from the horizontal, was to be painted NS Insignia White. (i.e. lower points of tangency).

The vertical or curved surfaces of the hull or fuselage, between the NS Sea Blue color of the upper surfaces and the NS Insignia White of the lower surfaces, were to be graduated in tone from the NS Sea Blue to the NS Insignia White by means of either of the following methods:

(A) By blending the two colors over the intervening area in such a manner that there was a gradual transition in the tone without noticeable demarcation between the colors. In any case, the tone of the curved surfaces, where

Scouting Squadron 41 Dauntless on deck of USS RANGER CV-4, during "Operation Torch", the invasion of French North Africa, November 1942. Yellow circle around national insignia was directed by an amendment to Operation Memorandum No. 9 dated 25 September 1942. In this document it was directed that all American aircraft taking part in "Operation Torch" apply this Yellow band to their national insignia on both sides of the fuselage and on both lower wing surfaces. (USN/National Archives)

Curtiss SBC-3, in camouflage paint, being towed to Anacostia, D.C. by PBY-5A for repairs to seized-up engine. (USN/National Archives via D. Bruce Van Alstine)

Close-up of SBC-3 engine cowling showing soft line of demarcation between top and bottom colors of camouflage paint. (USN/National Archives via D. Bruce Van Alstine)

they approached the vertical, was to be approximately that of the NS Intermediate Blue color.

(B) By the use of NS Intermediate Blue over the intervening area, blending into the two adjacent colors in such a manner that there was a gradual transition without noticeable demarcation between the colors.

On small fighters method A was preferred, however, on large flying boats method B was thought to be more practicable.

The areas of the hull or fuselage normally in the shadows cast by the horizontal airfoils, were to be counter-shadowed from NS Insignia White at the airfoil root by gradually darkening the tone until the paint was the same color as the adjacent fuselage areas. In no case, however, was pure NS Insignia White to extend beyond lines tangent to the leading and trailing edges of the airfoil root which were fifteen degrees from the horizontal (i.e., lines forming an acute angle with the wing).

Vertical surfaces of the rudder assembly and vertical fin were paintd with the NS Intermediate Blue color.

Floatplanes (OS2U, SOC, etc.) had their floats camouflaged with NS Sea Blue on the top surface down to the chine, and NS Insignia White on the bottom surface up to the chine. Camouflaged float struts were painted NS Intermediate Blue. The upper end of the large struts could be counter-shadowed if desired.

At this time, the coloration of propeller tips changed from the three 4 inch bands of Insignia Red - Orange-Yellow - Insignia Blue to a 4 inch band of Glossy Orange Yellow from tip to four inches from the tip.

Propeller spinners were usually painted NS Intermediate Blue on airplanes painted in the basic tri-color camouflage scheme. Some squadrons adopted personal colors for their spinners, (i.e., Air Group One on the USS Yorktown, CV-10, painted their spinners NS Willow Green during their tour in 1944)

Advanced training aircraft remained as per SR-51d as well as did primary training planes. Instrument flying aircraft retained their Green stripes as originally directed in February 1942. On wing surfaces, the fore and aft stripes were to be located an equal distance from each wing tip, and were to clear the national insignia. On the fuselage surface, the stripe was to be located between the aft edge of the fuselage insignia and the leading edge of the horizontal stabilizer.

At this time, the national insignia was removed from the top of the starboard wing and the bottom of the port wing.

The color of the markings (leters and numerals) depended on the color to which they were applied. The directive stated that NS Intermediate Blue was to be applied against a background of White or Dark Blue with Black being used on a background color of NS Intermediate Blue. Photographic evidence shows that in many cases, White letters and numerals were also used on USN planes.

PBY-5A unloading German POWs at Natal, Brazil in February 1943. Standard camouflage scheme of the time period with "83P7" in Black on forward section of hull. (USN/National Archives)

Brewster F2A-3 showing application of ANA-611 primer to inside surface of main landing gear. This color was used on all interiors of USN, USMC, and USCG aircraft after 22 December 1942. (USN/National Archives)

Tri-color paint scheme as directed by SR-2c in January 1943. Aircraft is Grumman TBF-1 on USS BUNKER HILL CV-17, 28 June 1943. (USN/National Archives via H. Andrews)

T-1 landing on BUNKER HILL, July, 1943. Underside of left wing shows former location of national insignia and wrap around of top surface color on leading edge. (USN/National Archives via H. Andrews)

Olive Green and Non-specular Light Grey Beech JRB-1, personal plane of Major General A. A. Vandergrift, Commanding General, 1st Marine Division. Photo taken at Essendon Airport, Melborne, Australia, 6 July 1943. First Division insignia and two-star placard are outstanding features of the General's plane. Basic camouflage paint scheme is not in USN specifications of the time. (USMC via R.P. Gill)

On training airplanes, the color of the letters and numerals were to be of the highest contrast to the background color.

Model designation and Bureau number-branch of service lettering remained on the rudder and vertical fin respectively. On all camouflaged aircraft, this marking was applied in one inch figures. On large flying boats, they were applied in 3 1/2 inch figures.

An interesting directive, Aer-E-2574-MVS, F39-1, 14708, issued on 30 January 1943, gave instructions on how to make the new colors directed in SR-2c. This directive was issued to help speed up the change over by using available paints to obtain the new colors through mixing, and to curb waste by utilizing existing stock on hand. The following directions were given for mixing the new colors from the old.

to make NS Sea Blue —

Blue Gray	6 parts by volume
Insignia Blue	4 parts by volume
Black	2 parts by volume
OR	
Dark Blue	4 parts by volume
Insignia Blue	5 parts by volume
Black	2 parts by volume
Insignia White	1 part by volume

To make Semi-Gloss Sea Blue	
NS Sea Blue	
(from either of	
the above blends)	3 parts by volume
Clear Dope	
or Lacquer	1 part by volume

To make NS Intermediate Blue	
Blue Gray	12 parts by volume
Insignia White	24 parts by volume
Dark Blue	2 parts by volume
Insignia Blue	1 part by volume
Insignia Red	1 part by volume

A note to the above stated that these formulas were only approximate, and were given only for guidance. It was further recommended that, when blending was carried out, small test batches be made and examined for conformance with the color standards, and for compatibility of ingredients, since different manufacturers' products may vary slighty from the standards. Also in this directive it was stated that training airplanes received painted in Army Air Force colors may be repainted in Navy colors at the discretion of the Commanding Officer of the unit receiving the airplane.

Specification SR-2d issued on 22 December 1943 with an effective date of 6 March 1944 was basically the same in content as SR-2c. The 22 December 1943 directive's major changes involved the following:

Camouflaged floats were to be painted NS Intermdiate Blue on top surfaces down to the chine. NS Insignia White on the bottom surfaces up to the chine, except on those portions which extended beyond the wings or fuselage and which would be exposed to view from above. These areas were to be painted NS Sea Blue.

The interior of the engine cowling on camouflaged airplanes were to be painted NS Black.

Ultra-high frequency and Very-high frequency antenna (rod type), could be painted Orange-Yellow if the CO of the unit so desired. Other types of

VB-20 SB2C-1C in tri-color paint scheme, 21 December 1943. (USN via W.T. Larkins)

VF-17 F4U-1 onboard BUNKER HILL during the carrier's shakedown cruise in 1943. Factory fresh tri-color paint is shown to good advantage as well as star-in-circle national insignia and Non-specular Insignia White fuselage coding. Squadron's insignia appears on engine cowling. (USN/National Archives.)

SB2C-1C Helldiver of VB-8 during training flight in December 1943. Pre-WW II style fuselage coding was usually abandoned when in the combat area. (USMC via R.P. Gill)

This XOSE-1 of the Edo Corporation displays tri-color camouflage as applied to floatplanes of the period. Main float propeller warning stripe consists of two parallel wavy lines, 1" wide and 3" apart, painted with Non-specular Insignia Red paint, from chine to chine. The included area is marked with the words "DANGER PROPELLER" applied in letters 2" high, using Red paint, at sufficiently frequent intervals to indicate the dangerous area. (W.T. Larkins)

Underside of SB2C's outer wing panels were painted Non-specular Intermediate Blue in order to blend with the rest of the airplane's visible surfaces when the wings were folded. Propeller spinner was to be painted Non-specular Intermediate Blue also. (Curtiss-Wright Corp. via W.T. Larkins)

antenna were to be finished in the basic camouflage scheme to match the adjacent parts of the airplane.

A coat of clear lacquer (glossy) was to be applied over the camouflage coat to an area approximately two feet in diameter surrounding exhaust stacks and oil drains. However, distinction was made that this clear glossy lacquer was to be used on White surfaces only.

The most notable change in exterior markings came about with the issuing of Amendment 1 to SR-2d dated 13 March, 1944.

This amendment specified that all previous Non-Specular paint application be changed to that of a gloss finish. As of this writing, proof of the adoption of the Glossy tri-color scheme has yet to be discovered through photographs or personal recollection. however, the authors feel that this order most certainly was complied with somewhere in the vast complex of World War II US Naval Aviation.

SR-2d's amendment 1 also stated that all fighter aircraft were to be painted Glossy Sea Blue over all exterior surfaces.

The size of squadron markings, numerals only, stayed the same as outlined in SR-2d: 16 inches for airplanes 50 feet or less in wing span; 24 inches high for larger than 50 foot wing span and, at the option of the CO, the squadron marking could be applied in figures 36 inches in height if the airplane's wing span were 100 feet or greater. These numerals were to be located on both sides of the vertical fin and rudder above the horizontal stabilizer. Single numbers were to be located close to the rudder hinge, while double numbers were to be located one on each side of the hinge. On multi-engined aircraft, the numbers were to be located immediately aft of the US national insignia.

NATIONAL INSIGNIA CHANGE

The first modification of our national insignia occurred during May of 1942. It was then that the Red disc was removed from the center of the White five pointed star. Pilots in the European Theater of Operations were the first to voice their opinions against the Blue and White star in circle insignia. There apparently were a great many instances when the pilots in the ETO found it difficult to distinguish our insignia from the Italian fasces on a solid field, the German Cross and the British Roundel. In answer to the objections growing around our star in circle design, an Orange-Yellow ring was placed

(Left) SB2C-4 noses over after landing mishap onboard USS CARD CVE-11 during carrier qualification trials in June 1944. Landing gear door numerals are 6" high per SR-2d and "14" on cowling is also 6" in height. (USN/National Archives)

PBY-5, in tri-color paint, makes jet assisted take-off. Good example of BuNo. and model designation being applied under horizontal stabilizer. (R. Minnear via W. T. Larkins)

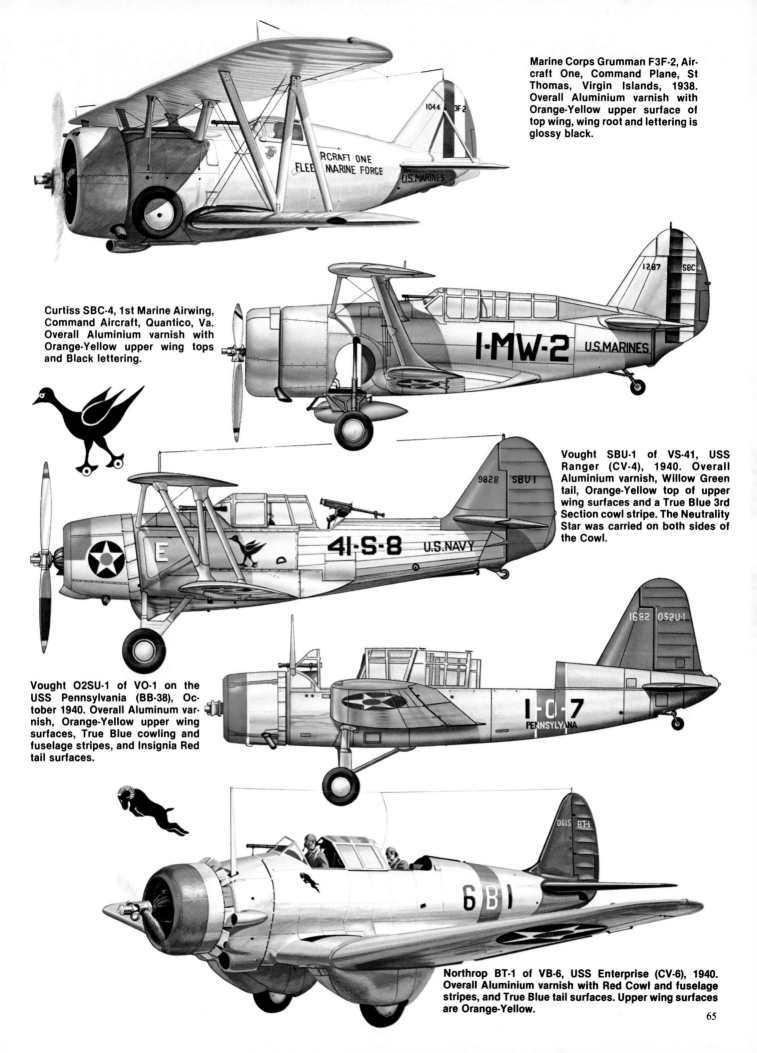

Marine Corps Grumman F3F-2, Aircraft One, Command Plane, St Thomas, Virgin Islands, 1938. Overall Aluminium varnish with Orange-Yellow upper surface of top wing, wing root and lettering is glossy black.

Curtiss SBC-4, 1st Marine Airwing, Command Aircraft, Quantico, Va. Overall Aluminium varnish with Orange-Yellow upper wing tops and Black lettering.

Vought SBU-1 of VS-41, USS Ranger (CV-4), 1940. Overall Aluminium varnish, Willow Green tail, Orange-Yellow top of upper wing surfaces and a True Blue 3rd Section cowl stripe. The Neutrality Star was carried on both sides of the Cowl.

Vought O2SU-1 of VO-1 on the USS Pennsylvania (BB-38), October 1940. Overall Aluminum varnish, Orange-Yellow upper wing surfaces, True Blue cowling and fuselage stripes, and Insignia Red tail surfaces.

Northrop BT-1 of VB-6, USS Enterprise (CV-6), 1940. Overall Aluminium varnish with Red Cowl and fuselage stripes, and True Blue tail surfaces. Upper wing surfaces are Orange-Yellow.

65

Grumman F6F-3 Hellcat in flight with tri-color paint scheme as directed by specification SR-2c of 5 January 1943. All surfaces viewed from above, with the exception of the fuselage, were to be painted Semi-gloss Sea Blue. All surfaces viewed from below were Non-specular Insignia White. Lighter shade between top surface color and undersurface color was Non-specular Intermediate Blue which extended aft to include the vertical tail surfaces, fin and rudder. White rectangles and Insignia Red outline of national insignia were added to national insignia by order of Specification AN-I-9a of 29 June 1943. (USN via H.S. Gann)

around our insignia. This style of insignia was worn by US Navy aircraft participating in th Invasion of French North Africa; Operation Torch - November 1942.

It soon became apparent that our national insignia would have to be changed. Two of the first designs tested by the Army Air Force Proving Ground Command at Elgin Field, Florida, consisted of a single Blue star bordered by a narrow band of White and Red, and later, two Blue stars on a White oval rimmed by a Red band. The last design tested, met with approval by all concerned. That design featured a five pointed White star centered on a circumscribed circle of Insignia Blue. Two Insignia White rectangles were added to the sides of the Blue circle, and placed in such a position that they formed a straight line with the two most outer points of the star forming a horizontal line with the top of the two White rectangles and the horizontal line of the star. The dimensions of the two rectangles were to be the same length as the radious of the Blue circle and 1/2 the radious in width. The en-

tire insignia was then outlined with a border of Insignia Red, 1/8th the width of the radious. This new style national insignia was introduced to the US Fleet on Army-Navy Specification AN-I-9a on 29 June 1943.

The new insignia was modified less than 4 months later, when the Insignia Red border was removed and replaced by a border of the same dimensions, but of a different color, Insignia Blue. Later when the Gruman F6F Hellcat began to appear from the factory in the overall Glossy Sea Blue paint scheme, the national insignia underwent an unofficial modification. For some reason, yet to be documented, the US national insignia as applied to the F6F did not carry the Insignia Blue circle or border. Most likely, this was a decision by the Navy representative at the factory as a measure to speed up the insignia application and save on the purchase of Insignia Blue paint. This style of applying the national insignia was peculiar to the Gruman factory, as the F4U, SB2C, TBM, and other non-Grumman models were delivered with the national insignia in it's entirety. The star and bar insignia outlined with the Blue border remained our standard aircraft insignia throughout the remainder of World War II.

VMF-123 F4U-1s on airstrip in Russell Islands, September 1943. Field modification of US national insignia is very evident in this photograph. Horizontal rectangles were added to star in circle design and Red outline omitted on F4U nearest camera. Second F4U, #101, has an outline around its national insignia while the third F4U in line-up has what appears to be a very light colored outline around its national insignia. The use of the star and bar insignia on the tops of both wings was non-standard at this time. (USMC via R.P. Gill)

RANGER based Dauntlesses enroute to attack German shipping in the Norwegian port of Bodo on 4 October 1943. RANGER SBDs and TBFs sank five ships and damaged seven others. RANGER's F4F's shot down two German aircraft during the raid. Standard tri-color paint and Red outlined national insignia with 20" tail number adorn these SBDs. (USN/National Archives

STANDARD LIST OF AIRCRAFT CAMOUFLAGE

Army-Navy Aeronautical Bulletin No. 157 of 28 September 1943 brought together under one heading, all the colors then in use, by the Army Air Forces and the Bureau of Aeronautics. This bulletin listed only the Non-Specular camouflage colors used by both services at that time. Then on 4 December, of the same year, a list of Glossy colors was issued under the designation ANA Bulletin No. 166.

The only modification made to the above lists during WW II came about on 24 March 1944, when ANA Bulletin No. 157a was issued. The nearest British equivalent colors were listed as well as those for which the AN standard colors may be substituted. Also the name of color 619 was amended to read "Bright Red" in place of "Insignia Red". These two colors are identical: Bright Red is Non-Specular and Insignia Red is Glossy.

VF-17 F4U-1s after national insignia change of 29 June 1943. Underside of Corsair's wings are Non-specular Intermediate Blue. (USN/National Archives)

ARMY — NAVY AERONAUTICAL BULLETIN NO. 157
of 28 SEPTEMBER 1943.

Color	Finish	ANA Number
Instrument Black	Semi-gloss	514
Insignia White	Non-specular	601
Light Grey	Non-specular	602
Sea Grey*	Non-specular	603
Black	Non-specular	604
Insignia Blue	Non-specular	605
Sea Blue	Semi-gloss	606
Sea Blue	Non-specular	607
Intermediate Blue	Non-specular	608
Azure Blue	Non-specular	619
Sky	Non-specular	610
Interior Green	Non-specular	611
Medium Green	Non-specular	612
Olive Drab	Non-specular	613
Orange Yellow	Non-specular	614
Middlestone	Non-specular	615
Sand	Non-specular	616
Dark Earth	Non-specular	617
Dull Red	Non-specular	618
Bright Red	Non-specular	619
Light Gull Grey**	Non-specular	620
Dark Gull Grey***	Non-specular	621

*Also known as Non-specular Blue Grey.
**Used in anti-submarine camouflage scheme.
***Used in anti-submarine camouflage scheme.

ARMY — NAVY AERONAUTICAL BULLETIN No. 166
of 4 DECEMBER 1943.

Color	Finish	ANA Number
Light Blue	Glossy	501
Insignia Blue	Glossy	502
Light Green	Glossy	503
Olive Drab	Glossy	504
Light Yellow	Glossy	505
Orange Yellow	Glossy	506
Aircraft Cream	Glossy	507
International Orange	Glossy	508
Insignia Red	Glossy	509
Maroon	Glossy	510
Insignia White	Glossy	511
Aircraft Grey	Glossy	512
Engine Grey	Glossy	513
Black	Glossy	515
Strata Blue	Glossy	516

Note: The color card supplement to U.S. Army Specification No. 3-1 of 21 April 1943, cross-references the color Light Blue to be the same as "True Blue", Light Yellow to "Lemon Yellow" and Light Green to "Willow Green", the pre-WW II U.S. Navy tail and section colors.

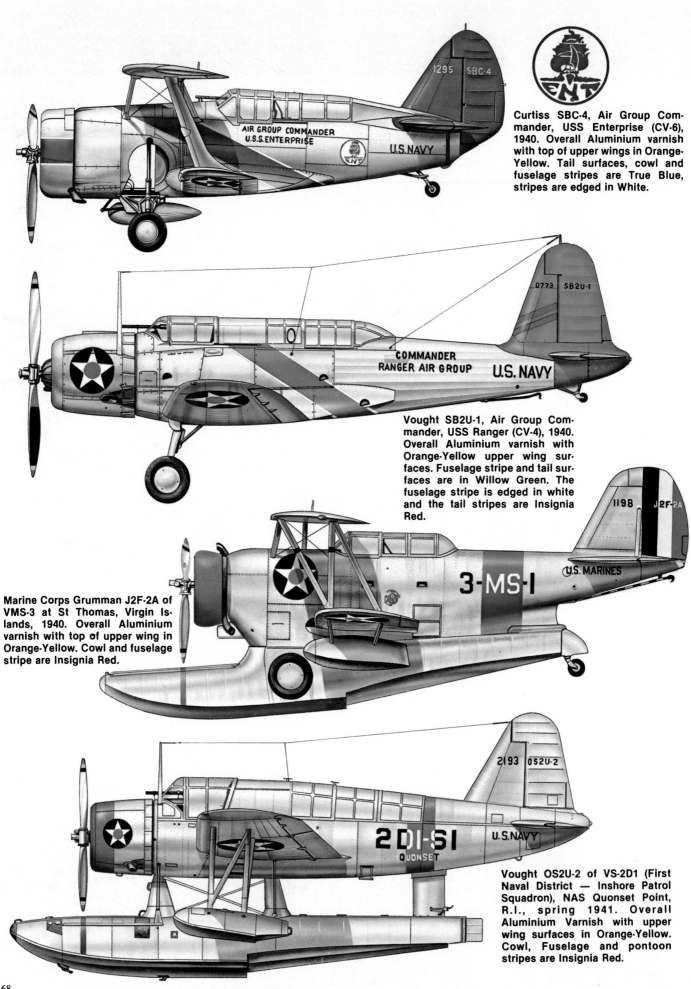

Curtiss SBC-4, Air Group Commander, USS Enterprise (CV-6), 1940. Overall Aluminium varnish with top of upper wings in Orange-Yellow. Tail surfaces, cowl and fuselage stripes are True Blue, stripes are edged in White.

Vought SB2U-1, Air Group Commander, USS Ranger (CV-4), 1940. Overall Aluminium varnish with Orange-Yellow upper wing surfaces. Fuselage stripe and tail surfaces are in Willow Green. The fuselage stripe is edged in white and the tail stripes are Insignia Red.

Marine Corps Grumman J2F-2A of VMS-3 at St Thomas, Virgin Islands, 1940. Overall Aluminium varnish with top of upper wing in Orange-Yellow. Cowl and fuselage stripe are Insignia Red.

Vought OS2U-2 of VS-2D1 (First Naval District — Inshore Patrol Squadron), NAS Quonset Point, R.I., spring 1941. Overall Aluminium Varnish with upper wing surfaces in Orange-Yellow. Cowl, Fuselage and pontoon stripes are Insignia Red.

Vought SBU-1s of Scouting Squadron 42 during 1940. Painted in overall Aluminium varnish and carrying the neutrality star as well as various color codings provide a rather colorful airfield scene. (USN)

Grumman J4F-1 of the US Coast Guard Station at San Francisco during 1941. V201 was not decommisioned until August 1947. The Coast Guard emblem is carried just below the window. (W T Larkins)

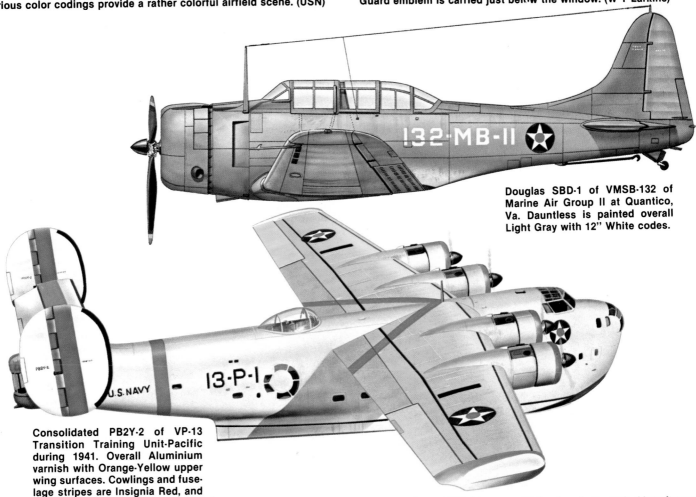

Douglas SBD-1 of VMSB-132 of Marine Air Group II at Quantico, Va. Dauntless is painted overall Light Gray with 12" White codes.

Consolidated PB2Y-2 of VP-13 Transition Training Unit-Pacific during 1941. Overall Aluminium varnish with Orange-Yellow upper wing surfaces. Cowlings and fuselage stripes are Insignia Red, and the tail stripe is True Blue.

A Douglas SBD-1 Dauntless of Marine Corps VMB-2 in a rare 1940 color photograph. Aircraft number one is always assigned to the squadron commander. (Douglas via H.S. Gann)

Grumman's first Bearcat with large letters "TEST" applied to the fuselage. Subject of photo, the XF8F-1, displays the US national insignia minus the circumscribed Blue circle and Blue outline. This style of national insignia application began with Grumman on the F6F Hellcat and finally received official sanction with the issuing of ammendment 1 to Specification An-I-9b on 10 June 1946. (Grumman A/C Engineering Co. via W. T. Larkins)

Another example of the word "TEST" being applied to an experimental aircraft is seen here. Grumman XF7F-1 Tigercat in overall natural metal finish with Glossy Orange-Yellow "TEST" outlined with a 1"Black border. (Grumman A/C Engineering Co. via W. T. Larkins)

SPECIFICATION SR-2e - June 1944

This final painting document of World War II, excluding two minor amendments issued between June '44 an VJ Day, was destined to be the basic specification for US Navy aircraft painting until 1947.

Specification SR-2e reinstated the Non-Specular finish for US combat airplanes of the patrol/patrol bombing, and observation and helicopter catagories.

With the issuing of this document, all USN carrier based aircraft were to be painted overall Glossy Sea Blue. However, many bombing and torpedo planes retained the tri-color basic camouflage scheme until the final day of fighting.

Land transports were to be finished overall Aluminum color while seaplane transports were to be painted in the overall Glossy Sea Blue scheme.

In the utility catagory, landplanes and amphibious types were to be finished overall Aluminum color with seaplane utility aircraft receiving the overall Glossy Sea Blue adornment.

Target-towing aircraft were painted overall Orange-Yellow.

Primary trainers still carried the overall Orange-Yellow scheme which made them famous as "Yellow Perils".

Advanced trainers of the landplane variety were to be painted overall Aluminum color, and seaplanes in this line were painted overall Glossy Sea Blue. Combat type seaplanes or landplanes used for training purposes were to be delivered in the color of the type.

Target drone aircraft were to be painted overall Glossy Insignia Red.

The "new" item in SR-2e centered around the anti-submarine aircraft camouflage scheme. This scheme was designed for use in areas where no enemy air opposition was to be expected. There were two schemes outlined in the directive as follows:

Scheme I - This scheme was designed for use in areas where the prevailing weather conditions were clear, clear with scattered clouds, or clear above with moderate surface haze:

Topside Surfaces	NS Dark Gull Gray
Side Surfaces	NS Light Gull Gray
Bottom Surfaces	Glossy Insignia White
Leading edges and Frontal Surfaces	NS Insignia White
Side Surfaces in shadow of horizontal airfoils: Side areas of huls, fuselage and nacelles under the wings and horizontal stablizers	NS Insignia White
Cowl openings: inside of cowling, reduction gear housing, propeller dome and propellers themselves out to inner edge of cowl opening	NS Insignia White

Scheme II — This sceme was designed for use in areas where the prevailing weather conditions were overcast. This scheme was also supposed to be the best to use during morning, evening twilight or night operations.

Summary of Scheme II:

Same as scheme I except that in scheme II, NS Insignia White replaced Light Gull Gray.

The propeller warning stripe stayed at 4 inches from tip toward the hub, but on propellers with a basic diameter of 15 feet or more, the warning stripe was to be painted from tip to 6 inches from the tip on both sides with Glossy Orange-Yellow paint.

Droppable fuel tanks were to be painted to match the adjacent surfaces of the airplane to which it was attached. Many NS Insignia White fuel tanks placed under the F6F Hellcat type soon took on a "Pinkish" hue as a result of aviation fuel contamination.

At this stage of World War II, carrier aircraft had been operating for quite some time with individual carrier air group markings painted on the fin and rudders of said aircraft. These markings were unofficial and some were even of a temporary nature. The designs then in use stayed with the air group regardless of the carrier they operated from during this time period. Air Group 20 flew from both the Enterprise and the new Lexington with their planes marked with their White triangle. SR-2e contains reference to this type of marking and also states that the marking could be applied with temporary identification paint of White, Yellow or Medium Green if desired. To date, the only known examples of coloring for these markings is White.

Near the end of 1944, the Bureau issued an amendment to SR-2e. In this amendment, Number One of 30 December, a new color scheme for patrol and patrol bombing aircraft was described.

All patrol and patrol bombing aircraft were to be painted as follows:
Top and bottom surfaces of wings and all horizontal tail surfaces - Semi-Gloss Sea Blue.
All other tail surfaces and the entire fuselage - NS Sea Blue.

All patrol and patrol bombing seaplanes and amphibians were to be painted in the basic Non-Specular camouflage scheme

Amendment 2 to SR-2e dated 10 March 1945, concerned the color of propeller blades and propeller hubs and domes. The remaining blade area was to be as before, NS Black. On training type aircraft, the front of the propeller blade did not have to be painted NS Black. All hubs and domes were to be painted Black, Non-Specular, except when the airplane was painted in the anti-submarine camouflage scheme. In that case, they were painted NS Insignia White.

PB4Y-2 with fancy mottled camouflage effect on fuselage and engine nacelles. This Privateer (59357) is a beautiful example of tri-color camouflage paint application. (Pratt & Whitney via W. T. Larkins)

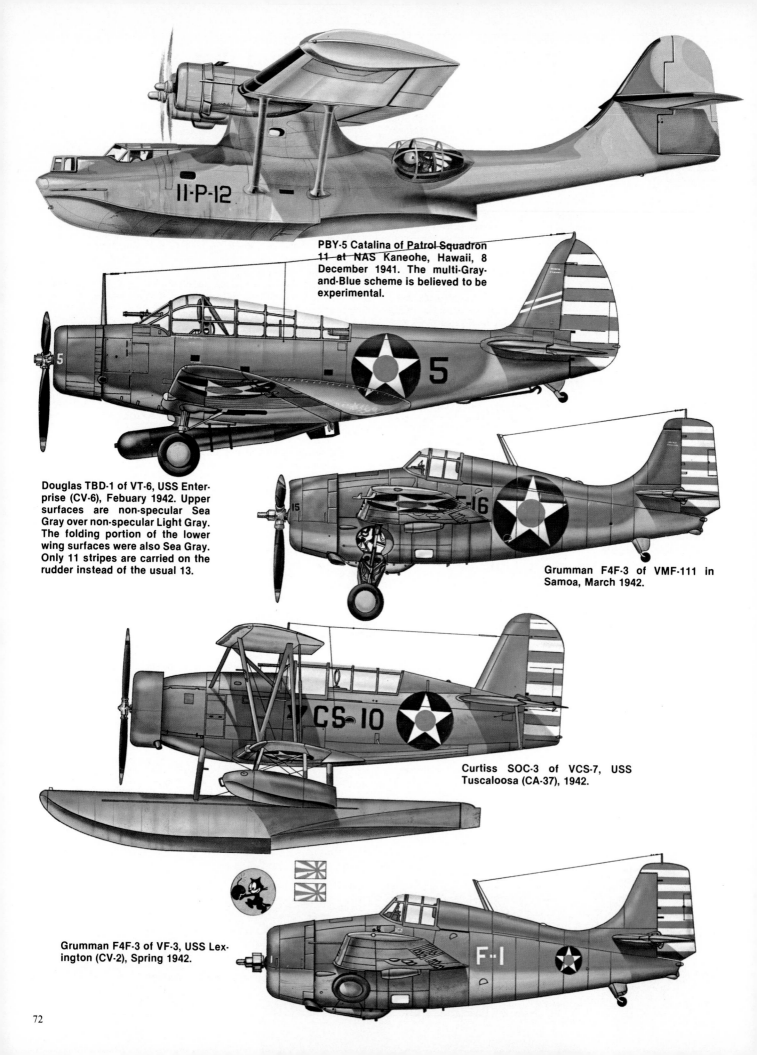

PBY-5 Catalina of Patrol Squadron 11 at NAS Kaneohe, Hawaii, 8 December 1941. The multi-Gray-and-Blue scheme is believed to be experimental.

Douglas TBD-1 of VT-6, USS Enterprise (CV-6), Febuary 1942. Upper surfaces are non-specular Sea Gray over non-specular Light Gray. The folding portion of the lower wing surfaces were also Sea Gray. Only 11 stripes are carried on the rudder instead of the usual 13.

Grumman F4F-3 of VMF-111 in Samoa, March 1942.

Curtiss SOC-3 of VCS-7, USS Tuscaloosa (CA-37), 1942.

Grumman F4F-3 of VF-3, USS Lexington (CV-2), Spring 1942.

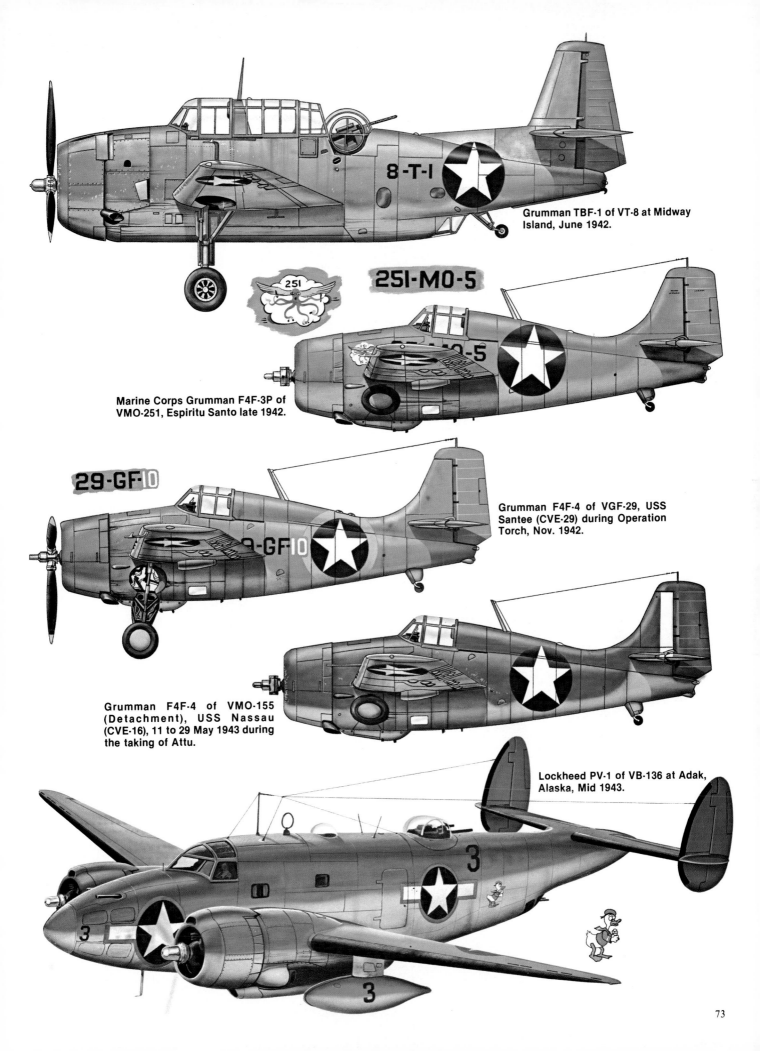

8-T-1

Grumman TBF-1 of VT-8 at Midway Island, June 1942.

251-MO-5

Marine Corps Grumman F4F-3P of VMO-251, Espiritu Santo late 1942.

29-GF-10

Grumman F4F-4 of VGF-29, USS Santee (CVE-29) during Operation Torch, Nov. 1942.

Grumman F4F-4 of VMO-155 (Detachment), USS Nassau (CVE-16), 11 to 29 May 1943 during the taking of Attu.

Lockheed PV-1 of VB-136 at Adak, Alaska, Mid 1943.

Top view of PB4Y-2 carrying tri-color scheme. (Consolidated Aircraft via W. T. Larkins)

Lockheed PV-2 patrol bomber illustrates basic camouflage scheme for it's type in late 1944. Blue outlined national insignia are seen to good advantage. (Lockheed Aircraft Co. via G. Nikola)

Factory-fresh Curtiss SB2C-5. Use of Non-specular Sea Blue anti-glare panel forward of the cockpit canopy is to be noted. The last three digits of the Helldiver's BuNo. as an ID number during delivery can be seen applied in White on the nose of the aircraft. Overall paint scheme is Glossy Sea Blue per SR-2e of 26 June 1944. (Curtiss-Wright Corp. via W. T. Larkins.)

Howard GH-2 utility plane shows unusual placement of BuNo on rudder. This land based transport type aircraft was painted overall Aluminum in accordance with SR-2e. (USMC via R.P. Gill)

Budd RB-1 (39294) Conestoga, stainless steel transport, in it's natural state did not require Aluminum paint per SR-2e as did other types of land transports. Later many RB's were painted in tri-color camouflage paint which did little or nothing for it's ungainly appearance. (Pratt & Whitney Aircraft via W.T. Larkins)

Case in point...Tri-colored RB-1, enough said. (USN via M.J. Kishpaugh)

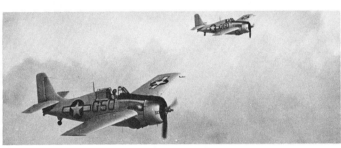

General Motors FM-2 advanced trainers in their overall Aluminum paint scheme. Non-specular Black or Medium Green anti-glare panel can be observed as well as large "G50" and "G60" fuselage codes. These codes were to be applied with Black paint if the background was White or Aluminum. (R. Minnear via H.S. Gann)

Beech GB-2 with station name applied to forward fuselage. NAS Vero Beach, Florida later became the spring training headquarters for the major league baseball Dodgers.(Cdr. H.S. Packard, USN, Ret.)

Grumman J2F-5 and Douglas SBD-1 at Moffett Field, California, 1943 (W Reed)

Douglas SBD-5s on the line at the Douglas factory during the summer of 1943. Red outlined national insignia adopted for use on 29 June 1943. The tri-color scheme is seen to good advantage. (Douglas via Harry Gann)

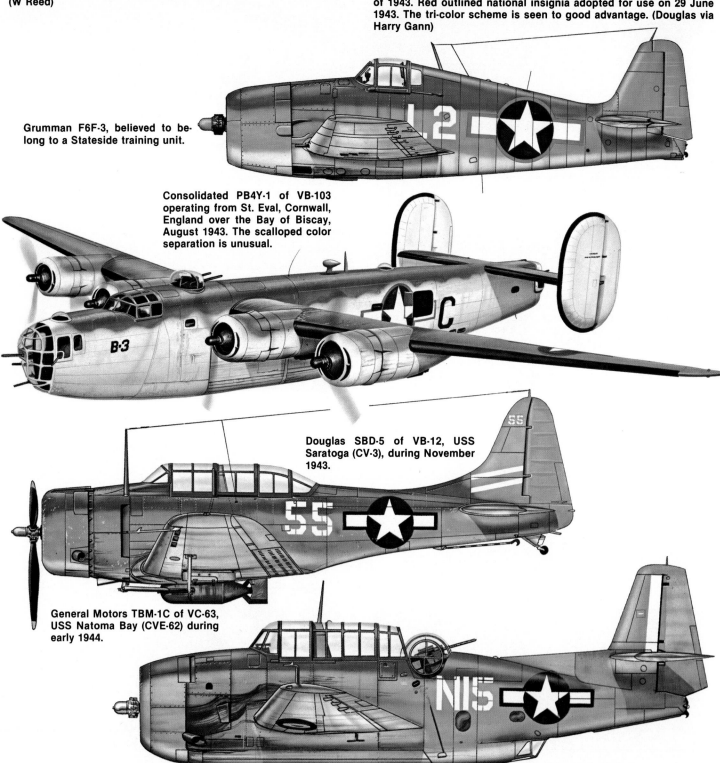

Grumman F6F-3, believed to belong to a Stateside training unit.

Consolidated PB4Y-1 of VB-103 operating from St. Eval, Cornwall, England over the Bay of Biscay, August 1943. The scalloped color separation is unusual.

Douglas SBD-5 of VB-12, USS Saratoga (CV-3), during November 1943.

General Motors TBM-1C of VC-63, USS Natoma Bay (CVE-62) during early 1944.

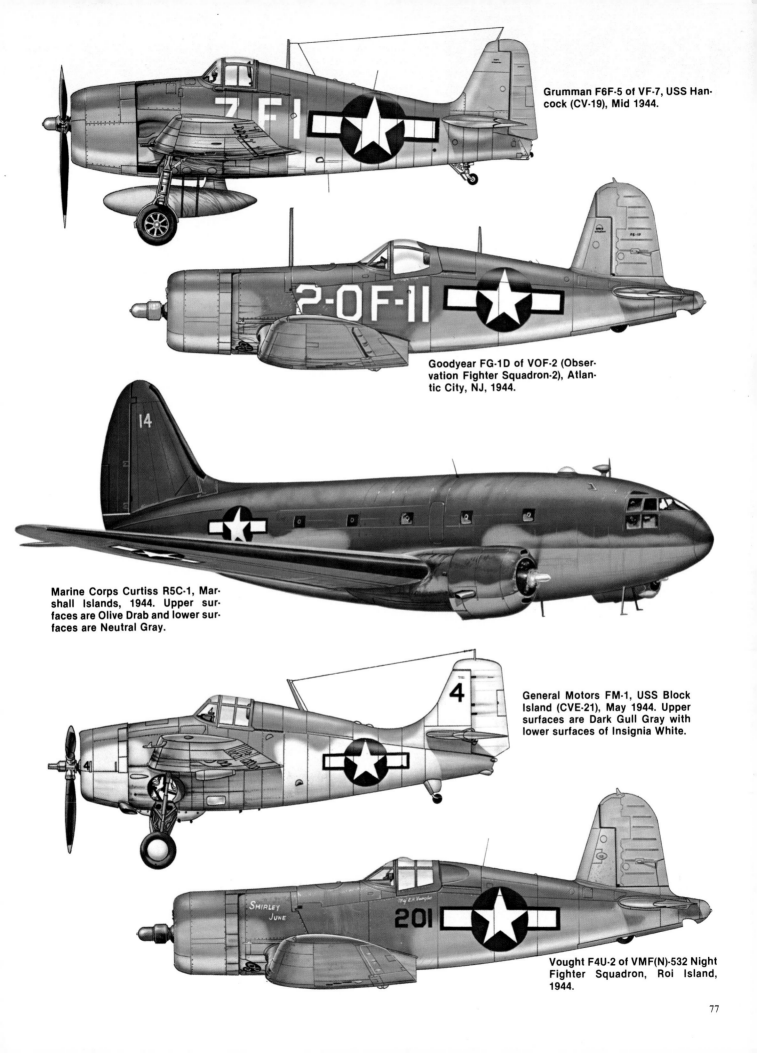

Grumman F6F-5 of VF-7, USS Hancock (CV-19), Mid 1944.

Goodyear FG-1D of VOF-2 (Observation Fighter Squadron-2), Atlantic City, NJ, 1944.

Marine Corps Curtiss R5C-1, Marshall Islands, 1944. Upper surfaces are Olive Drab and lower surfaces are Neutral Gray.

General Motors FM-1, USS Block Island (CVE-21), May 1944. Upper surfaces are Dark Gull Gray with lower surfaces of Insignia White.

Vought F4U-2 of VMF(N)-532 Night Fighter Squadron, Roi Island, 1944.

This General Motors (Eastern Division) FM-1 carries the low-visibility Atlantic Theater anti-submarine paint scheme #2, adopted for USN carrier planes with the issuing of Specification SR-2e on June 1944. Top color is Non-specular Dark Gull Grey; side color, including tail surfaces is Non-specular Insignia White; bottom color is Glossy Insignia White. This GM Wildcat displays Insignia Blue outline around national insignia as directed in Specification An-I-9b of 14 August 1943. (USN/National Archives)

Composite Squadron (VC) Nine FM-2 on USS SOLOMONS, CVE-67, in June 1944. Anti-sub scheme #2. (USN/National Archives)

General Motors TBM-1D "Night Owl" Avenger in flight on 24 October 1944. Night flying TBMs had extra fuel tanks which enabled them to stay in the air longer during their search for German submarines. The TBMs operated as the "hunter" while the F4Fs were the "killer" part of the CVE based teams. (VD-2 via W.T. Larkins)

Navy version of Liberator bomber, PB4Y-1, shows anti-sub scheme #2. Line of demarcation on this England based PB4Y is very definite while on other aircraft types it is very soft. Red outlined national insignia is carried. (USN/National Archives)

Sikorsky HNS-1 helicopter during training flight at Floyd Bennett Field, Brooklyn, in November 1943. This HNS-1 (46445) carries Red outlined national insignia. Camouflage on helicopter is presently unknown. In October 1944, SR-2e directed all helicopters to be painted in the basic camouflage scheme for landplanes and patrol aircraft. At this point, November 1943, helicopters were not listed in the painting documents. It appears that a light shade of paint is on the underside of this HNS-1, possibly Non-specular Light Grey. The top color is belived to be Non-specular Medium Green, Olive Drab or Sea Blue. Coast Guard had three HNS-1s at Floyd Bennett Field in November 1943. (USCG)

(Below) Coast Guard rescue demonstration held in 1944. HNS-1 is from Floyd Bennett Field. Pilot is Cdr F.A. Erickson and man in U-type rescue harness is AMM 1/c Carl A. Yanuzzi, USCG. (USCG)

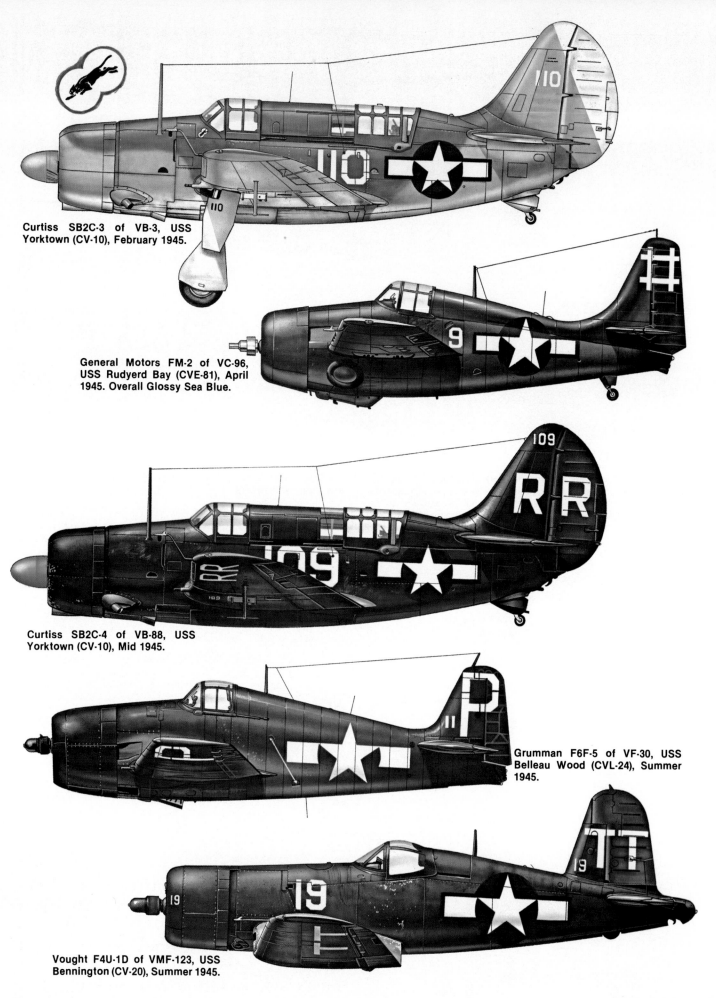

Curtiss SB2C-3 of VB-3, USS
Yorktown (CV-10), February 1945.

General Motors FM-2 of VC-96,
USS Rudyerd Bay (CVE-81), April
1945. Overall Glossy Sea Blue.

Curtiss SB2C-4 of VB-88, USS
Yorktown (CV-10), Mid 1945.

Grumman F6F-5 of VF-30, USS
Belleau Wood (CVL-24), Summer
1945.

Vought F4U-1D of VMF-123, USS
Bennington (CV-20), Summer 1945.

PB4Y-1 (32059) showing the soft line demarcation on this type aircraft in the application of anti-sub scheme #2. Aft rectangle of national insignia is painted over plexiglass window in fuselage. (USMC via R.P. Gill)

Anti-submarine scheme #1 showing use of Non-specular Light Gull Grey applied to the side of this long range PB4Y-1. Underside coloring, White, is visible on aft fuselage. (USN/National Archives)

VP-211 PBM-3S from the Navy base at Galeao, Brazil, on patrol over Rio Harbor March 1944. Anti-sub scheme #2 with Light Grey and Blue national insignia on hull. (USN/National Archives)

1945 TAIL MARKINGS - "G" SYMBOLS - TAIL LETTERS

To standardize the system of tail markings, the Bureau issued a set of standard designs in Air Force, Pacific Fleet, Confidential Letter No. 2CTL-45, FF 12-5/F39-2/Ro, serial number 06040 dated 27 January 1945.

Tail markings for purposes of identification during World War II actually began in 1942 when seven Red and six White horizontal rudder stripes were utilized. However, tail markings used to identify specific air groups began in late 1943. This system, while workable, presented the risk of similarity and duplication because it was not controlled nor standardized by official documentation.

The markings alloted to the CV's and CVL's had no exact dimensions, but were to be applied to the vertical tail surfaces and wing surfaces per the examples that accompanied the official letter. Individual airplane numbers were to be applied on the tail surface in such a manner that they did not interfere with the basic design of the identification marking. These markings were applied with Insignia White paint over the background color.

On 7 February 1945, the commander of Task Force 58, Marc Mitscher,

issued a letter to the Commander First Carrier Task Force, Pacific, directing that the markings issued on 27 January be employed as soon as possible. This letter, File No. F13, serial 047, also stated that the Commander of Task Group 58.5 was authorized to adopt different markings for his carriers' if he so desired. Note should be made that Saratoga, Yorktown and Wasp modified their original design as set forth in the 27 January directive, and Enterprise adopted a completely different design from the one originally assigned to CV-6. On 29 March, Captain G.B.H. Hall informed the commander of Task Force 58 that he was assigning a design to his aircraft that he believed reduced their visibility during night operations. His carrier was operating as a night carrier at that time with an all night flying air group aboard. The design favored by Captain Hall featured a forward pointing spearhead outlined in White. He did not want the design applied on the wings and, as an anti-searchlight measure, he had the White star and bar national insignia on the bottom of the starboard wing oversprayed with a water soluble Gray paint. Captain Hall's letter was filed under the designation CV6/F39(95-k1), serial number 140.

Numerical designations of air groups began in 1942. The first being Carrier Air Group 9, commissioned 1 March 1942. The earliest known Air Group using identifying tail markings was the diagonal vertical fin stripe of Air Group 5. This Air Group 5 F6F-3 belongs to the group's commander. "In the field" tri-color paint application is evident. Also of note is the small Red outlined national insignia, and double zero side number which designates the Air Group Commander's aircraft. (USN/National Archives)

Same marking as Air Group 5, but in this case it is Air Group 1. When Air Group 5 finished it's tour, aircraft and ID markings were taken over by Air Group 1 which flew from USS YORKTOWN CV-10 in 1944. Plane is a TBF-1C. (USN/National Archives)

"G" Symbol chart given to pilots operating from fast carriers. Below is a replica of the chart carried by Ensign Stan Brown of VT-27 off USS Independence CVL-22 in 1945.

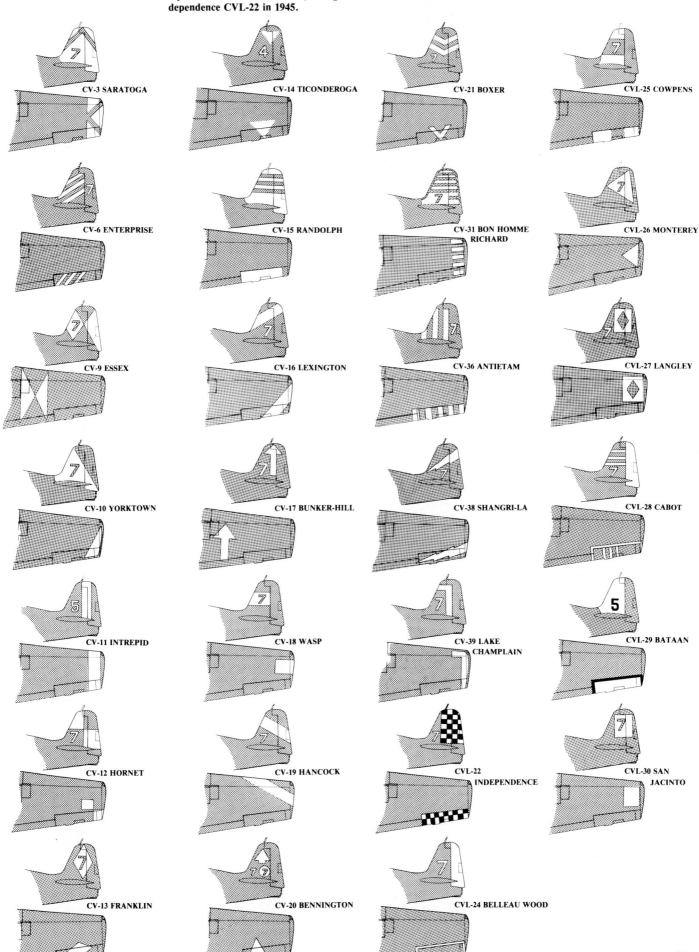

CV-3 SARATOGA   CV-14 TICONDEROGA   CV-21 BOXER   CVL-25 COWPENS

CV-6 ENTERPRISE   CV-15 RANDOLPH   CV-31 BON HOMME RICHARD   CVL-26 MONTEREY

CV-9 ESSEX   CV-16 LEXINGTON   CV-36 ANTIETAM   CVL-27 LANGLEY

CV-10 YORKTOWN   CV-17 BUNKER-HILL   CV-38 SHANGRI-LA   CVL-28 CABOT

CV-11 INTREPID   CV-18 WASP   CV-39 LAKE CHAMPLAIN   CVL-29 BATAAN

CV-12 HORNET   CV-19 HANCOCK   CVL-22 INDEPENDENCE   CVL-30 SAN JACINTO

CV-13 FRANKLIN   CV-20 BENNINGTON   CVL-24 BELLEAU WOOD

F6F-3 of Air Group 2, VF-2, USS HORNET CV-12, mid-1944. (USN/National Archives)

SB2C-3E of Air Group 7, VB-7, USS HANCOCK CV-19, during late 1944. (USN/National Archives)

SB2C-1C of Air Group 8, VB-8, USS BUNKER HILL CV-17, during mid-1944. (USN/National Archives)

TBF-1C of Air Group 14, VB-14, USS WASP CV-18, during mid-1944. (USN/National Archives)

(Below) Air Group 15, VF-15, USS ESSEX CV-9, during mid-1944. Aircraft is an F6F-3 (THE MINSI) belonging to Cdr. David McCampbell, and carried the letters "AGC" on the landing gear doors. (USN/National Archives)

Air Group 19, VF-16, USS LEXINGTON CV-16, during mid-1944. The Group's F6Fs did not carry ID marking on tail. Instead they applied a large individual aircraft number on the fuselage directly behind rear window of canopy. (USN via J. Consiglio)

(Below) TBM-C of Air Group 19, VT-16, USS LEXINGTON CV-16 during mid-1944. (USN/National Archives)

F6F-5s of Air Group 20, VF-20, USS ENTERPRISE CV-6, during late 1944. (USN/National Archives)

(Right) F6F-5 of Air Group 22, VF-22, USS COWPENS CVL-25, during late 1944. (USN/National Archives)

(Below) F6F-3 of Air Group 29, VF-29, USS CABOT CVL-28, during late 1944. Left wing of F6F is still painted Non-specular Sea Blue with a Glossy Sea Blue aileron. Undoubtedly a replacement wing. (USN/National Archives)

F6F-5N of Night Air Group 41, VFN-41, USS INDEPENDENCE, CVL-22, during late 1944. (USN/National Archives)

F6F-5 of Air Group 44, VF-44, USS LANGLEY CVL-27 late 1944. (USN/National Archives)

TBM-1C of Air Group 51, VT-51, USS SAN JACINTO CVL-30, during mid-1944. (USN/National Archives)

(Right) SB2C-3 of Air Group 80, VB-80, USS TICONDEROGA CV-14, during late 1944. (USN/National Archives)

Example of late WW II victory flag application on Cdr. David McCampbell's F6F-5 "MINSI III". He finished war with 34 confirmed aerial victories. (USN/National Archives)

Non-specular Intermediate Blue used on the leading edge of the wing was non-standard. Non-specular Sea Blue was the correct color called for in this area. The balance of the wing was to be Semi-gloss Sea Blue. Aircraft is TBM-3 of VMTB-233 onboard the first all-Marine carrier, USS BLOCK ISLAND CVE-106. February 1945. (USMC via R.P. Gill)

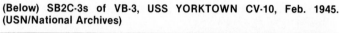

(Below) SB2C-3s of VB-3, USS YORKTOWN CV-10, Feb. 1945. (USN/National Archives)

(Above) After January 1945, the carrier air group markings gave way to Carrier Identification symbol ("G" symbols) which identified the carrier to which the aircraft were assigned as opposed to the identification of just the air group. These symbols consisted of various geometric designs and were applied with Glossy Insignia White to one or both ailerons and the tail surfaces of the aircraft. The outlined arrow design was adopted by the USS ENTERPRISE CV-6. This was not the original design assigned CV-6 by the Bureau. (USN/National Archives)

(Below) F4U-1D of VBF-10 off USS INTREPID CV11, April 1945. This Corsair carries a Lightning Bolt "G" symbol (SHANGRI LA) on the underside of left wing, indicating that it had, at one time, been on that carrier. (USN via W. T. Larkins)

(Above) F6F-5 of VF-83, USS ESSEX CV-9, April 1945. (USN/National Archives)

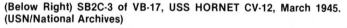

(Below Right) SB2C-3 of VB-17, USS HORNET CV-12, March 1945. (USN/National Archives)

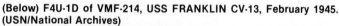

(Below) F4U-1D of VMF-214, USS FRANKLIN CV-13, February 1945. (USN/National Archives)

SB2C-4Es of VB-12, USS RANDOLPH CV-15, May 1945. (USN/National Archives)

F4U-1D of VMF-221, USS BUNKER HILL CV-17, March 1945. Nose band is Glossy Orange-Yellow. (USN/National Archives)

F4U-1D of VBF-86, USS WASP CV-18, February 1945. Non-standard numbers on WASP tail band were common to WASP aircraft at this time. (USN/National Archives)

TBM-3 of VT-46, USS INDEPENDENCE CVL-22, March 1945. Checker design appeared on both top and bottom surfaces of starboard aileron. (S. Brown)

F6F-5s of VF-22, USS COWPENS CVL-25, January 1945. (USN/National Archives)

F4U-1D of VMF-112, USS BENNINGTON CV-20, February 1945. (USN/National Archives)

F6F-5 of VF-47, USS BATAAN CVL-29, APRIL 1945. (USN/National Archives)

SB2C-5s and F4U-4s lined up on the deck of the USS ANTIETAM CV-36, during mid-1945. (USN/National Archives)

SB2C-5 off USS LAKE CHAMPLAIN CV-39, during mid-1945. (USN/National Archives)

SB2C-3E of VB-6, USS HANCOCK CV-19, April 1945. White propeller spinner of note. (USN/National Archives)

Photo Liberator, PB4Y-1, of VD-1, in the air near the island of Iwo Jima, early 1945. Tri-color scheme on PB4Y-1s was not very common at this stage of the war. Noteworthy is the extreme wear on the wing leading edges. (W.C. Munkasy)

HAWAIIAN SEA FRONTIER MARKINGS

A little known identification system governing naval aircraft operating in the Hawaiian Islands came into being in February 1945. On 11 February a directive A3/FF12-5/(112tr, serial 3133) was issued to mark all carrier and training type aircraft with an identification letter followed by an individual aircraft numeral from 1 to 99. These letters and appropriate numbers were to be placed on the aircraft by the Carrier Aircraft Service Units (CASU's) making sure that the aircraft based on the field are numbered without duplication.

The letters and numbers were to be 36 inches high, White if on a dark background, Black if on an Aluminum or light background, and located on the underside of the port wing and both sides of the fuselage. In the event fuselage size did not permit the placing of letters 36 inches in height, the letters/numbers were to be as near 36 inches as possible.

Letters assigned were as follows:

CASU-2 Barbers Point	A,B,C,D,E,F,
CASU-38 Kaneohe	G,H,
CASU-1 Ford Island	I,J
CASU-32 Puunene	O,P,Q
CASU-31 Hilo	R,S,T
Marines Ewa	U,V,W,

Compliance to this order was given as of 1 March 1945.

On 18 February 1945, a letter was sent from the CO of CASU-1 informing the Commanding Officers of the following squadrons of their letter and number assignments.

Letter I — CASU-1 No. 1 to 94 inclusive
      NAS Pearl Harbor (operations)
      No. 95 to 99 inclusive
Letter J — VS-53 No 1 to 19, inclusive
      VS-69 No 20 to 39 inclusive
      VS-46 No 40 to 59 inclusive
      Open No 60 to 65 inclusive
      VS-69 No 66 to 69 inclusive
      Open No 70 to 99 inclusive

All carrier types were to be maked as directed. this included the F6F, FM, F4U, SB2C, SBD, TBF and TBM.

Multi-engined aircraft, JRB, JRF, J4F, and SNB were exempt from this directive.

Training types, SNV and SNJ were covered.

Markings on the fuselage were not to be any smaller than 18 inches and a dash (-) was to be located between the letter and the number for better visibility.

An interesting letter, written on 24 February 1945, by the Commander Hawaiian Sea Frontier to the Commander Air Force, Pacific Fleet, stated that since VS-46, 53 and 69 were engaged in anti-submarine patrol, it was his opinion that the ID letters and numbers assigned would defeat the purpose of the camouflage effect of the basic tri-color paint scheme.

The Hawaiian Sea Frontier commander did not want to apply the markings to his anti-submarine aircraft and so stated in writing in letter S28, serial 443.

The reply from Commander Air Force, Pacific Fleet, informed the Commander Hawaiian Sea Frontier that the purpose of marking the HSF aircraft was to facilitate their identifcation after numerous reports of violations of air discipline by US naval aircraft. These violations involved aircraft flying too close to transport aircraft and ground installations.

The letter went on to say that since the aircraft's national insignia further upset the camouflage scheme, in addition to the letters and numbers, and the actual effectiveness of aircraft camouflage was in question, Commander Hawaiian Sea Frontier's request was denied. The ID letters and numbers would be applied as directed.

On 22 March 1945, the next to final wartime report regarding HSF aircraft was sent to Commander Air Force, Pacific Fleet. According to the letter, F3-2 serial 114, the Commanding Officer of Scout Observation Service Unit Number One (SOSU-1) had been assigned the letter/numbers I-90, I-91, I-92 and I-93 for aircraft in his custody.

The last known report concerning wartime markings of the HSF was issued on 10 June 1945. In the letter, F3-2, serial 202, a re-assignment of letter/numbers was given. Effective as of 10 June 1945, CASU-1 was assigned the numbers 1 to 89 inclusive; SOSU-1 the numbers 90 to 99 inclusive; numbers 1 to 89 were un-assigned and NAS Pearl Harbor would be assigned numbers 90 to 99 inclusive.

Thus ends the Hawaiian Sea Frontier adventure, at least for the time being.

Planes operating in the Hawaiian Islands area, the so-called Hawaiian Sea Frontier (HSF), were letter coded to identify the bases from which they operated. These F4Us carry the letter "W" to indicate MCAS Ewa. This lettering system, for HSF aircraft, began in February 1945. Aircraft in the photo are painted overall Glossy Sea Blue per SR-2d's Ammendment 1 of 13 March 1944. Color of nose cowling is White. (USMC via R.P. Gill)

TAIL AND WING LETTERS

As the war moved on into the summer of 1945, the Bureau decided to design and issue a set of tail and wing identification markings for aircraft operating from escort carriers, CVEs. On 2 June, Air Force, Pacific Fleet, Confidential Letter No. 4 CTL-45 was distributed to all concerned parties operating in the Pacific combat area. Prior to the 2 June 1945 order, the Pacific CVEs were using a non-standard system of carrier identification markings on their aircraft. These markings (see chart) were assigned to carriers operating with Carrier Divisions 22 through 27. Some of the markings were shown on the original chart as being applied in a color other than White. It is the authors' assumption that the "other color" could have been Light Yellow or Light Green, as both colors were mentioned earlier in SR-2e for use in the application of identification markings.

Meanwhile in the battleship navy....

There were probably more identification marking directives issued during 1945 than any year since the very beginning of US Naval Aviation. Following close on the heels of the 2 June CVE ID directive, the Commander of Battleship Squadron One issued an order, FC1-1F39, serial 817, on 9 July 1945, which was intended to effect a uniform numbering system for all aircraft attached to the ships of Battleship Squadron One.

Block numerals in White were to be painted on either side of the aircraft's fuselage, midway between the trailing edge of the wing and the forward edge of the insignia. These numerals were to be 14 inches by 10 inches in size. The width of the stroke was to be 2 inches with 2 inch spacing.

The numbers painted on each aircraft consisted of the number of the battleship division to which the parent ship was attached, together with a second number which was the individual number of the aircraft itself. An example of the numbering system in use would be — The USS Tennessee, flagship of Battleship Division Two, would have numbered it's aircraft 21 and 22. The USS New Mexico, third ship in Battleship Division Three, would have numbered it's aircraft 35 and 36.

The geometrical design system of aircraft identification adopted by the Fleet in January 1945 was not working out as well as had been expected. Admiral John S. McCain, Commander of Task Force 38, was responsible for the discontinuance of the "G" symbol ID system. In a dispatch written on 27 July 1945 Admiral McCain expressed his desire that the "G" symbols be dropped and an easier to remember system of tail and wing letters be adopted. The dispatch, No. 061121, stated that the "G" symbols were not intelligible visually and they were hard to describe over voice circuits.

The tail and wing letters were to be located on the top right and on the bottom left wings near the tip, and on both sides of the upper part of the rudder. They were to be White block letters (capital) 2 feet high. The dispatch listed the letters assigned to each carrier. They were as follows:

USS Saratoga, CV-3	CC
USS Ranger, CV-4	PP
USS Enterprise, CV-6	M
USS Essex, CV-9	M
USS Yorktown, CV-10	RR
USS Intrepid, CV-11	E
USS Hornet, CV-12	S
USS Franklin, CV-13	LL
USS Ticonderoga, CV-14	V
USS Randolph, CV-15	L
USS Lexington, CV-16	H
USS Bunker Hill, CV-17	Y
USS Wasp, CV-18	X
USS Hancock, CV-19	U
USS Bennington, CV-20	TT
USS Boxer, CV-21	ZZ
USS Independence, CVL-22	D
USS Belleau Wood, CVL-24	P
USS Cowpens, CVL-25	A
USS Monterey, CVL-26	C
USS Langley, CVL-27	K
USS Cabot, CVL-28	R

On 2 June 1945, CVE based aircraft were issued a set of standardized tail and wing ID markings. Shown here are TBM-3s from USS CAPE GLOUCESTER CVE-109. Tail marking was Glossy Insignia White and fuselage bands were Glossy Willow Green. Designs were repeated on top of starboard wing and bottom of port wing. (USN/National Archives)

USS Bataan, CVL-29	T
USS San Jacinto, CVL-30	B
USS Bon Homme Richard, CV-31	SS
USS Antietam, CV-36	W
USS Shangri La, CV-38	Z
USS Lake Champlain, CV-39	AA
USS Midway, CVB-41	YY
USS Franklin D. Roosevelt, CVB-42	FF
USS Coral Sea, CVB-43	EE

This system of aircraft identification proved to be the best. Over 30 years after the adoption of tail and wing letters, the US Navy still uses the system started by Admiral McCain in 1945. The carriers have changed since then, but the alphabet has, and will remain the same.

In a follow-up letter of 27 August 1945, C2CTF/F39, serial 01614, Admiral McCain reported that the letter system of identification was working fine, but that experience indicated that the tail and wing letters should be 30 to 36 inches in height and that numerals should be removed from the tail surfaces of Fleet aircraft and moved to the fuselage to eliminate any chance of confusion.

Enter the CVEs once again....

In September 1945, additional CVEs began operating with the Pacific Fleet. On 3 September, a set of ID markings was issued to cover the 12 escort carriers then beginning operations. The letter, Air Force, Pacific Fleet, Confidential Technical Letter No. 8CTL-45, FF-12-5/39-2, (WW-15-rc), serial 06312, was meant to be a supplement to the 2 June 1945 CVE ID marking document. (See chart for 3 September 1945 CVE ID system).

Even though the Second World War officially ended on 2 September 1945, at least one more identification system was put into effect for aircraft operating in the Hawaiian Islands area.

On 10 September, letter No. A3/FF12-5/ (112-Cs), serial 19030, was issued, assigning a set of identification letters to the air stations in the Hawaiian Islands area. These letters were to be 36 inches high, White if on a dark background, Black if on an Aluminum or light background, and were to be located on the underside of the port wing and both sides of the fuselage. The appropriate letters were followed by a number from 1 to 99 inclusive. In the event that all available numbers in the 1 to 99 bracket were utilized, and no additional letters were available, the use of numbers over 100 was authorized.

Only aircraft assigned to a station were affected, pool aircraft were not to be marked in any way. The letter assignments were as follows:
(CASU - Carrier Aircraft Service Unit)

Barbers Point	CASU-2	A-B-C-D-E-F-Y
Kaneohe	CASU-38	G-H
Ford Island	CASU-1	I
Ford Island	Utility Wing	J-U
Kahului	CASU-32	K-L-M-N
Puunene	CASU-4	R-S-T
Hilo	CASU-31	R-S-T
Ewa	Marines	V-W-Z

The ID markings outlined in the 10 September 1945 letter were to be applied to station aircraft by 1 October 1945.

The most demanding period of United States Naval Aviation history came to a close in late 1945. The time span, 1941 to 1945, brought great change to our nation's way of life. Everyone old enough to remember will not deny the tragedies of that war. Naval Aviation played a very important part in World War Two, sacrifice and hard work were the main factors. A very small but significant factor was the color and markings of our Navy's aircraft. There is really no way to measure the success of the various color and markings systems used during the first 44 years of our Navy's involvement with airplanes. Surely during times of war, ID systems are important and if just one life was saved because of these systems then this small but significant factor becomes very important indeed. We now bring to an end volume one, we hope your understanding of the subject has been enhanced, we hope you've enjoyed it.

Tail and wing identification letters began appearing after the 27 July 1945 directive, CTF Dispatch #061121, was issued. Most carriers were able to change over to the new system within a relatively short time. Thus examples of the old "G" symbol system can be seen along with the new lettering system. Shown here is an SB2C-4 from the USS TICONDEROGA CV-14 with the letter "V" visible on the vertical tail surface of the aircraft. (USN/National Archives)

F6F-5s of VF-16, USS RANDOLPH CV-15, August 1945. (USN/National Archives)

F6F-5N of VFN-91 off USS BON HOMME RICHARD CV-31, September 1945. (USN/National Archives)

F6F-5 of VF-27, USS INDEPENDENCE CVL-22, VF-27, August 1945. (USN/National Archives)

SB2C-4 on the deck of USS LEXINGTON CV-16, August 1945.(USN/National Archives)

F6F-5 off USS SHANGRI LA CV-38, August 1945. (USN/National Archives)

Example of carrier-based aircraft still painted in tri-color scheme during the closing days of WW II. This TBM-3 of VT-27, off the INDEPENDENCE, was flown by Ensign Stan Brown. (S. Brown Collection)

(Left) TBM-3 off USS MONTEREY CVL-26, August 1945. Girlie art on carrier based aircraft was extremely rare. (USN/National Archives)

Individualistic carrier identification design appears on tail of this VMF-511 F6F-5N Hellcat. White block with Blue "I" indicates the carrier USS BLOCK ISLAND CVE -106. Small letter "M" signifys Marines. BLOCK IS- LAND was first all-Marine carrier in Pacific, during early 1945. CVE individual designs became history with the 2 June 1945 standardized CVE ID markings directive. (USN/National Archives)

95

CVE (Escort Carrier) Identification Markings
Issued 2 June 1945

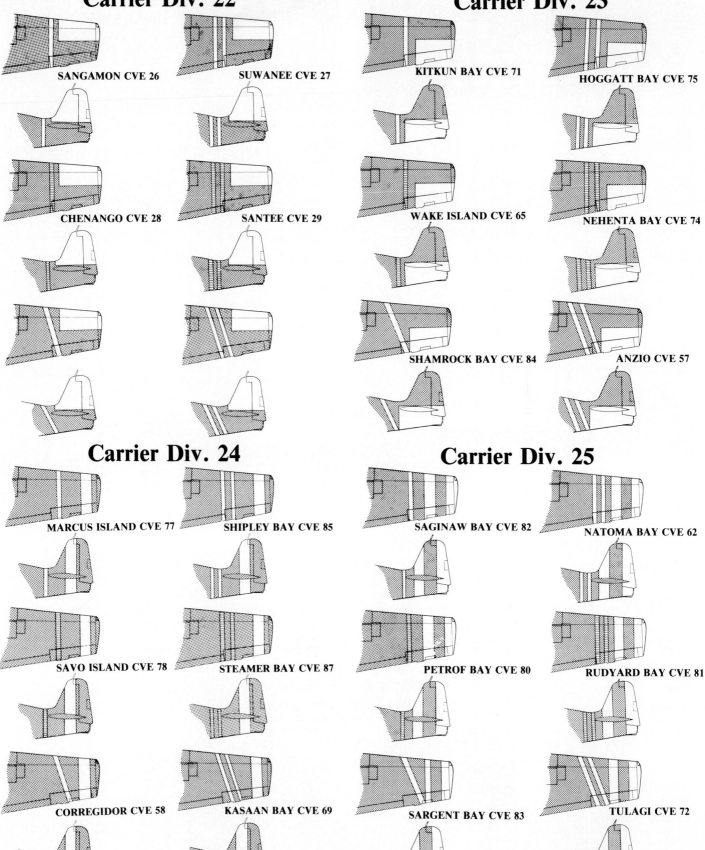

Carrier Div. 22

SANGAMON CVE 26

SUWANEE CVE 27

CHENANGO CVE 28

SANTEE CVE 29

Carrier Div. 23

KITKUN BAY CVE 71

HOGGATT BAY CVE 75

WAKE ISLAND CVE 65

NEHENTA BAY CVE 74

SHAMROCK BAY CVE 84

ANZIO CVE 57

Carrier Div. 24

MARCUS ISLAND CVE 77

SHIPLEY BAY CVE 85

SAVO ISLAND CVE 78

STEAMER BAY CVE 87

CORREGIDOR CVE 58

KASAAN BAY CVE 69

Carrier Div. 25

SAGINAW BAY CVE 82

NATOMA BAY CVE 62

PETROF BAY CVE 80

RUDYARD BAY CVE 81

SARGENT BAY CVE 83

TULAGI CVE 72

YELLOW